P9-CFN-924

50 LITERACY STRATEGIES
for *Culturally Responsive* Teaching, K-8

WITHDRAWN

50 LITERACY STRATEGIES
for *Culturally Responsive* Teaching, K-8

TOURO COLLEGE LIBRARY
Kings Hwy

WITHDRAWN

Foreword by Lee Gunderson

Patricia Ruggiano Schmidt & Wen Ma

CORWIN PRESS
A SAGE Publications Company
Thousand Oaks, California

KH

Copyright © 2006 by Corwin Press

All rights reserved. When forms and sample documents are included, their use is authorized only by educators, local school sites, and/or noncommercial or nonprofit entities who have purchased the book. Except for that usage, no part of this book may be reproduced or utilized in any form or by any means, electronic or mechanical, including photocopying, recording, or by any information storage and retrieval system, without permission in writing from the publisher.

For information:

Corwin Press
A Sage Publications Company
2455 Teller Road
Thousand Oaks, California 91320
www.corwinpress.com

Sage Publications Ltd.
1 Oliver's Yard
55 City Road
London EC1Y 1SP
United Kingdom

Sage Publications India Pvt. Ltd.
B-42, Panchsheel Enclave
Post Box 4109
New Delhi 110 017 India

Printed in the United States of America

Library of Congress Cataloging-in-Publication Data

Schmidt, Patricia Ruggiano, 1944-
50 literacy strategies for culturally responsive teaching, K–8/Patricia
Ruggiano Schmidt and Wen Ma.
      p. cm.
Includes bibliographical references and index.
ISBN 1–4129-2571–1 (cloth)—ISBN 1–4129–2572-X (pbk.)
   1. Language arts (Elementary)—Activity programs. 2. Multiculturalism—Study and teaching—Activity programs. 3. Literacy. I. Ma, Wen. II. Title.
III. Title: Fifty literacy strategies for culturally responsive teaching, K–8.
LB1576.S3255 2006
796.323'63'0973—dc22   2006001769

This book is printed on acid-free paper.

06   07   08   09   10   9   8   7   6   5   4   3   2   1

Acquisitions Editor:	Jean Ward
Editorial Assistant:	Jordan Barbakow
Copy Editor:	Bill Bowers
Typesetter:	C&M Digitals (P) Ltd.
Proofreader:	Teresa Herlinger
Indexer:	Rick Hurd
Cover Designer:	Scott Van Atta

6/23/06

Contents

Foreword

Patricia Ruggiano Schmidt and Wen Ma are to be congratulated for writing what will become a classic and invaluable classroom resource, *50 Literacy Strategies for Culturally Responsive Teaching, K–8*. There is no more compelling rationale for this book than the teacher's comment quoted by the authors that "I'm an American; I don't have a culture." Many teachers are culturally out of contact with themselves and their roots. As I noted in 2000 in the *Journal of Adolescent and Adult Literacy*, teachers are ". . . the individuals of the third-, fourth-, and fifth-generations who are the lost ones whose first cultures like unsettled spirits haunt their angst-filled reveries. They are the shadow diasporas, consensually self-validated as groups, but only vaguely." How can a teacher address cultural issues and hold the belief that some human beings do not have a culture? It is with great excitement and expectation that I read this book. Schmidt and Ma state that ". . . we were inspired to design a text for elementary and middle education that demonstrates how to develop cultural sensitivity and an appreciation for differences." They also argue that much of what teachers know about culture and diversity amounts to stereotypes. I noted in 2004 that "The morning newspapers regale us with stories about illegal immigrants, immigrants who are criminals, and immigrants who become outstanding success stories, winning spelling bees or making vast fortunes." This book will help students and teachers get past the stereotypes. Bravo!

This book is a welcome addition to work in culture and diversity. It presents teaching and learning strategies designed to introduce students to the diversity in their own classroom communities. Strategies are designed for students who are beginners, intermediates, and advanced. The authors brilliantly connect their strategies to other areas of the curriculum.

I believe that what is most outstanding about this book may be an unintended, but significant, outcome. Students will learn about diversity and culture, but the most important outcome, I believe, will be that the teachers themselves will learn about the diversity and cultures in their own classrooms and schools by virtue of using the strategies. I have argued that if students' cultures are not considered by teachers, the students will fail. The pattern of failure across the United States appears to support this conclusion. This book provides multiple strategies for teaching students about diversity and culture. It is my hope that these strategies will help in some small way to reduce the number of students who feel alienated because their cultures are not recognized or are subject to stereotypical perceptions by their classmates and teachers.

Thank you to Schmidt and Ma for this gold mine of strategies. It is needed and overdue.

—Lee Gunderson
University of Vancouver, British Columbia, Canada
Past President of the National Reading Conference

Preface

WHY IS THIS TEXT NEEDED?

We, the authors of *50 Literacy Strategies for Culturally Responsive Teaching, K–8*, saw a great need for this text in our nation's schools. (Together we have 30 years of public school classroom teaching experiences and an additional 20 years in teacher education and research.) We discovered this need as we began talking with teachers and teacher educators across our country and working with our graduate and undergraduate students. Present and future elementary and middle school teachers appeared to be aware of our nation's ethnic, cultural, and linguistic diversity, but they expressed concerns about the lack of appropriate strategies and resources for differentiating instruction for these students in urban, rural, and suburban classrooms. Therefore, we were inspired to develop a literacy strategies text that emphasized cultural sensitivity and an appreciation for diversity, and that promoted literacy learning at elementary and middle schools. We see the concept of culture as the factor that embraces all kinds of diversity. For example, if the culture that surrounds linguistic or economic diversity is not addressed, how can we make the English language arts relevant? At first, we were hesitant about dealing with such a huge and complex task. But because of the unmet need, we decided that we must do something. As the medical profession pledges, "First, do no harm," we believed we must start somewhere. As a result, we state, honestly, that this text is not comprehensive; it is just an early attempt to assist teachers as they implement culturally responsive instruction.

WHAT IS THE PURPOSE OF THIS TEXT?

The purpose of this text is to help present and future teachers begin to make home/school/community connections that promote our students' academic and social achievement. All strategies connect to the English Language Arts Standards proposed by the International Reading Association (IRA) and the National Council of Teachers of English (NCTE) (Appendix A) and the standards will be noted in the introduction of each strategy. Many of these literacy strategies are not new, but are simply modified for culturally responsive instruction, thus demonstrating that making learning culturally relevant is not a great hurdle. We have also avoided too much specificity, since teachers traditionally adapt what they teach to their own students' specific strengths and challenges. Rarely do teachers implement strategies in exactly the same way each year.

WHERE HAVE APPLICATIONS
OF STRATEGIES OCCURRED?

We have repeatedly observed the application of most strategies in numerous elementary and secondary urban, high-poverty classrooms, so one could say that the strategies have been tested for success. A few teachers have adapted them for high school, and a few teachers in suburban and rural settings have successfully used them in their classrooms. These teachers realize that diversity exists in all populations. (Actually, every family has its own special culture: its own way of talking, working, celebrating, playing, etc.) The teachers ranged in professional experience from novice to 25 years and were willing to try these strategies simply because they were curious about them, frustrated with present teaching/learning results, and/or desired to encourage more successful literacy development. They recognized the time-consuming aspects of some strategies, but their efforts yielded the positive results that motivated them to continue with adaptation and application. Interviews and anonymous surveys revealed comments that have been inserted at the end of several strategies. We thought that these would be informative and encouraging.

WHAT ABOUT STEREOTYPICAL THINKING?

We realize that stereotypical understandings of certain groups of people can be strongly embedded in the psyche and that it is no easy task to change attitudes. But we believe that most teachers are predisposed to the negation of harmful stereotypes and want all students to achieve emotionally, socially, and academically in their classrooms. Moreover, we think we have seen that successful applications of the strategies may actually reinforce positive cultural sensitivity and might even begin to eliminate negative notions about certain groups of people.

WHO WILL FIND THIS TEXT USEFUL?

Inservice teachers will find *50 Literacy Strategies for Culturally Responsive Teaching, K–8,* particularly useful since it offers literacy strategies with transformative messages that can be used across the curriculum. According to English standard dictionaries, "a strategy is a carefully devised plan to achieve a goal or the art of developing or carrying out such a plan." Preservice teachers will also find this text useful as they practice teaching and designing literacy lessons.

HOW MUCH TEACHER EDUCATION
IS NECESSARY TO USE THESE STRATEGIES?

This unique text may encourage teachers to use culturally responsive strategies in their classrooms on Monday morning. We know that teachers appreciate an understanding of the theoretical foundations for particular strategies, so that they will be better prepared to implement them. Often, however, there is little time to discuss theory when there are pressing classroom requirements. Actually, the application of strategies helps teachers begin to think differently about differences, seeing first hand how they can be adapted to fit the needs of particular students. The very act of planning strategy application promotes communication between home, school, and community, thus strengthening connections for relevant instruction. Additionally, translators, sign language, and basic personal contacts promote relationships for English Language Learner (ELL) student success.

WHY EMPHASIZE CULTURAL DIFFERENCES?

Our focus is on cultural differences, since we believe that they have been ignored too long in favor of the dominant mainstream culture that empowers the European American and middle class population at the expense of the human dignity of the traditionally ignored peoples. It is "nice" to address similarities in classrooms. Doing so serves an important unifying purpose, but similarities are not what cause wars and serious disturbances in our world. Therefore, learning to value differences in perspectives, languages, cultures, physical appearances, and so forth, offers opportunities to expand inquiry learning, critical thinking, and problem solving (Siegler & Alibali, 2005). We have also included strategies related to differences in climate, geography, measurement, architecture, and flora and fauna. These differences demonstrate the evolution of human diversity and help us appreciate other cultures by bringing new ideas to our own.

Some strategies do not specifically and directly address certain groups, but will certainly assist in recognizing their enriching differences in the classroom. These strategies will assist in building learning communities that not only foster an appreciation of differences, but also promote reading, writing, listening, speaking, and viewing through meaningful activities. Additionally, these strategies may allow teachers to individualize and accommodate across different categories of special learner needs, such as students with academic, social, cognitive, emotional, physical, linguistic, and ethnic differences. All can participate and learn.

WHAT IS THE ORGANIZATION OF THE TEXT?

There are six major sections in this text. The first section is entitled Classroom Community: Getting to Know Me, Myself, and Us. It contains strategies to develop a risk-free learning community, one that offers a comfort level for sharing. Students in such classrooms are confident that their questions, answers, and contributions will be thoughtfully and respectfully responded to in ways that assist in the learning process for all. So we think these strategies may be useful at the beginning of the school year. However, any of these strategies may be repeated throughout the school year, as reminders and reinforcement for the importance of diverse learning communities, communities that support their members for understanding the curricula.

The next section, Home, Community, and Nation: Making Contributions to Literacy Learning, has strategies that can be interspersed throughout the school year whenever appropriate. We feel these strategies can be used again and again, with slight modifications, as students begin to see how important it is to connect with their home, community, and nation.

The third section, Multicultural Literature Events: Motivating Literacy Learning in Content Areas, is meant to do just that, with rich pieces of youth literature. The literature resources given as examples are presented to entice teachers to explore the many literature resources that exist to promote understanding of particular subjects in a content area. The List of Cited Youth Literature provided at the end of the book serves as an additional resource. These pieces of literature are successful motivators for culturally responsive lessons, since they represent numerous cultures. They are written and illustrated by authors and illustrators from diverse backgrounds.

The next section is Critical Media Literacy: Exploring Values. Today's youth are exposed to the media for many hours daily. Therefore, we believe it is essential to include culturally responsive strategies that encourage youth to critically analyze visual and print messages. These strategies may help students consider and think critically about stereotypes, fads, and biased news presentations.

The fifth section is Global Perspectives and Literacy Development: Understanding the World View. This group of strategies presents the *big picture*. Students are provided with opportunities to situate themselves and their cultures on the planet Earth. Activities related to the strategies help students see their own lives in relation to the lives of people from other parts of the world. The purpose of these literacy strategies is not only to help students deepen understanding of the curriculum, but also to extend their learning beyond local and national communities.

The last section is Inquiry Learning and Literacy Learning: Beginning to Know Research. The theme for this group of strategies is "questioning is the answer." School students learn early on that "the teacher asks questions and students give expected answers." Unfortunately, this is the structure of numerous classrooms throughout the world. However, in a democratic society, a questioning citizenry is what keeps democracy alive (Dewey, 1916; Herber, 1978; Schon, 1987). Therefore, it is the work of the educator to stimulate questioning behaviors and an inquiring spirit. These strategies will help students begin to take risks and ask questions and learn basic research procedures.

HOW DO I USE THIS TEXT?

Each strategy in *50 Literacy Strategies for Culturally Responsive Teaching, K–8* is presented to encourage easy implementation and adaptation to suburban, urban, and rural student populations in numerous curriculum content areas. Most strategies are presented with a brief explanation, links to the ELA (English Language Arts) Standards, and then steps to follow for beginning, intermediate, and advanced learners. Some strategies combine beginning and intermediate levels and others combine intermediate and advanced levels. For most strategies, materials are suggested and examples given. Furthermore, the strategies are not so prescriptive that the experienced teacher will feel as though she or he is following a script. The authors actually hope the strategies stimulate critical analysis and creative thinking. So, we encourage teachers to modify and extend lessons with more appropriate ideas and activities. At the end of each strategy, suggestions for curriculum connections are provided to assist in a broad-view, thematic learning process. Hopefully teachers will seize these opportunities to integrate and collaborate for connections across the curriculum and grade levels.

Please note that each strategy is connected to the IRA and NCTE Standards for the English Language Arts. Notice that teacher comments accompany many strategies as experienced "words of wisdom." These helpful comments may alert you to specific aspects in the implementation process.

Teachers may wish to begin at the beginning of this text, since the first two sections, Classroom Community: Getting to Know Me, Myself, and Us and Home, Community, and Nation: Contributions to Literacy Learning, focus on building strong learning communities and positive connections between home, school, and community. However, we also think that any of the strategies in different sections may be used in any order, as long as the classroom teacher integrates the strategy with a particular instructional goal or curriculum focus.

A word of caution is necessary here. Sometimes, communication with families and communities can be challenging when teachers are attempting to develop working relationships. So, the following tenets may be helpful to remember:

- Many teachers have discovered that sending notes home is the least effective way to contact families.
- Many teachers have discovered that personal phone calls and meetings on neutral ground, such as those at a recreation center, park, or local coffee shop, are most useful for initiating relationships with family and community members.
- Many teachers know that an interpreter-translator may be necessary for those new to this country who are learning our culture and the English language. Even though some people may appear to have a high level of English language proficiency, they may not understand the nuances of the culture. Therefore, interpreters-translators may be necessary for communication between home and school for those new to the English language as well as those new to the culture.

The key idea to remember is that the environment for sharing and collaboration must be *risk-free*, a place to begin positive and carefully attentive communication.

To begin using the strategies, teachers may prefer experimentation, so they might study strategies, find one that seems appropriate to the curriculum, and try it. The following directions may help.

- Read the first paragraph that describes the strategy.
- Then study the steps for beginner, intermediate, and advanced learning. These three levels are arbitrary at best. Beginners might be defined as kindergarten through second-grade interest and/or academic abilities. Intermediate might be defined as third- through fifth-grade interest and/or academic abilities, and advanced may be described as sixth- through eighth-grade interest and/or academic abilities. Additionally, some strategies are labeled *beginner/intermediate* and/or *intermediate/ advanced.* These were designed in this manner to indicate that the steps may be appropriate for both levels.
- Decide what level would be most appropriate for specific students in your class.
- Decide what can be accomplished by the whole class, what can be accomplished by small groups, and what can be accomplished by pairs or individual students.
- For English Language Learners who were good students in their native lands, pairing with an equal-ability student will maintain interest levels. If the student has had little formal education, the interest level is key. In both cases, drawing upon the positive memories of students' native lands and cultures is the first consideration. Students must be assisted in their comfort and interest levels to motivate them (Cummins, 1986; Igoa, 1995; Schmidt, 1998a, 2002).
- Family and community surveys, notes, or other written communication may need to be translated. Oral communication may also require translators. However, personal efforts to communicate with sign language can be effective when there is a sincere person-to-person effort put forth by the teacher.
- Study the curriculum connections to see how activities for the strategy can be integrated into particular content areas.
- Follow the steps, but always be open to modifying and adjusting to your students' interests and challenges.
- Finally, don't give up after one strategy doesn't seem to work. Try another . . . and don't worry about perfection. The strategies were created to produce a "healthy hum" (Schmidt, 2001, p. 141) in classrooms where reading, writing, listening, speaking, and viewing are used as powerful learning tools.

WHY IS THIS TEXT SO IMPORTANT?

This section is included as a brief theoretical framework and rationale for this text. The list of citations is referenced in the back of this text, so that educators may study more in-depth research.

The U.S. Department of Education predicts that by the year 2010, minority populations will become the majority populations in our schools (U.S. Department of Education, 2000). Presently, this diversity has had a significant impact on urban education, but in the future, will have an even greater impact on rural and suburban education. Therefore, it is time for successful teacher inservice and preservice programs to connect home, school, and community with culturally relevant or culturally responsive teaching (Au, 1993; Cochran-Smith, 1995; Florio-Ruane, 1994; Moll, 1992; Noordhoff & Kleinfield, 1993; Osborne, 1996; Schmidt, 2002, 2003, 2004, 2005; Tatum, 1992, 1997; Tatum, 2000; Willis & Meacham, 1997; Zeichner, 1993).

Research and practice demonstrate that strong home, school, and community connections not only help students make sense of the school curriculum, but also promote literacy development (Au, 1993; Boykin, 1978, 1984; Edwards, 2004, 1996; Faltis, 1993; Goldenberg, 1987; Heath, 1983; Leftwich, 2002; McCaleb, 1994; Moll, 1992; Reyhner & Gracia, 1989; Schmidt, 2000, 2004, 2005; Xu, 2000b). However, in recent years home, school, and community connections have become a significant challenge.

There are various reasons for this situation. First, as our school population has become increasingly diverse, both culturally and ethnically, our teaching population has consistently originated from European American, suburban experiences. Typically, educators describe themselves as white and middle class and often add, during discussions about diversity, "I'm an American; I don't have a culture." (Paley, 1989; McIntosh, 1990; Florio-Ruane, 1994; Snyder, Hoffman, & Geddes, 1997; Schmidt, 1999a). Second, most teachers have not had sustained relationships with people from different ethnic, cultural, and socioeconomic backgrounds. As a result, much of their knowledge about diversity has been influenced by media stereotypes (Finkbeiner & Koplin, 2002; Pattnaik, 1997; Tatum, 1997). Third, school curriculum, methods, and materials usually reflect only European American or white culture and ignore the backgrounds and experiences of students and families from lower socioeconomic levels and differing ethnic and cultural backgrounds (Boykin, 1978, 1984; Moll, 1992; Foster, 1994; Ladson-Billings, 1994, 1995; Delpit, 1995; Purcell-Gates, L'Allier, & Smith, 1995; Nieto, 1999; Howard, 2001; Sleeter 2001; Walker-Dalhouse & Dalhouse, 2001). Fourth, many teacher education programs do not adequately prepare educators for "culturally relevant pedagogy" (Ladson-Billings, 1995) a term that directly relates to making strong home, school, and community connections (Wallace, 2000; Sleeter, 2001; Lalik & Hinchman, 2001). Fifth, when cultural differences are ignored in classrooms, student fears and alienation increase (Cummins, 1986; Igoa, 1995; Schmidt, 1998a, 2002; Greene & Abt-Perkins, 2003). Consequently, this disconnect has become a national problem whose influence has been linked to poor literacy development and extremely high dropout rates among students from urban and rural poverty areas (Au, 1993; Banks, 1994; Cummins, 1986; Edwards, 2004; Edwards, Pleasants, & Franklin, 1999; Goldenberg, 1987; Heath, 1983; Nieto, 1999; Payne, DeVol, & Smith, 2005; Schmidt, 1998a, 1999b; Trueba, Jacobs, & Kurtin, 1990).

It is obvious that there is a significant body of research concerning culturally responsive teaching. Unfortunately, there has been little evidence of its implementation in our nation's schools. So, it seems appropriate to suggest that this text, offering culturally responsive literacy strategies, is not only needed, but also, as some would say, "urgently necessary."

ACKNOWLEDGMENTS

This book of strategies is the result of urban, rural, and suburban teachers who believed they could make a difference in the academic and social lives of their students. They volunteered for our inservice programs and enrolled in teacher education classes with us. They took the challenges we offered and applied them to the challenges in their own classrooms. They broke new ground in modern education by deferring, in some instances, to traditional educational practices of long ago . . . meeting with families outside of school. They visited in homes, parks, recreation centers, churches, mosques, and many other locales. Additionally, these elementary and middle school teachers demonstrated a genuine respect by using family and community resources in classrooms and schools. The teachers encouraged family and community members to contribute their "funds of knowledge" to schools, thus making the curriculum relevant to children's ethnic, cultural, and linguistic diversity.

We must thank these teachers for their bravery in attempting many ideas, and their creativity in adapting them in new ways.

Finally, we thank our editor, Jean Ward, for her vision and her belief in social justice.

Corwin Press gratefully acknowledges the contributions of the following reviewers:

Lori Czop Assaf
Assistant Professor
Texas State University–San Marcos
San Marcos, TX

Sandra Golden
Education Recruitment Specialist
Notre Dame College
South Euclid, OH

Barbara Kapinus
Senior Policy Analyst and Program Consultant
National Education Association
Washington, DC

Elizabeth Noll
Associate Dean for Graduate Programs,
Faculty Development & Associate Professor of Language,
    Literacy, & Sociocultural Studies
College of Education University of New Mexico
Albuquerque, New Mexico

Brenda A. Shearer
Professor of Reading Education
University of Wisconsin–Oshkosh
Oshkosh, WI

Doris Walker-Dalhouse
Professor of Reading
Minnesota State University Moorhead
Moorhead, MN

About the Authors

After more than 20 years of teaching in public schools, **Patricia Ruggiano Schmidt** completed her doctoral studies in Reading and Language Arts at Syracuse University. Her dissertation, *Cultural Conflict and Struggle: Literacy Learning in a Kindergarten Program*, was recognized by the International Reading Association and was published by Peter Lang. As a Professor of Literacy at Le Moyne College, she teaches courses in the elementary and secondary programs and has developed a model known as the ABC's of Cultural Understanding and Communication. This model is implemented around the world and helps elementary and secondary teachers communicate and connect with families and communities, and design culturally responsive literacy lessons. Recently Dr. Ruggiano Schmidt was the recipient of the International Reading Association's Elva Knight Research Award. This work has promoted the study of links between literacy learning and culturally responsive teaching in urban and rural elementary and secondary schools.

Presently, Dr. Ruggiano Schmidt lives with her husband, Tom, beside a small lake and golf course in East Syracuse, New York.

Wen Ma completed his doctoral study in English Education at the University at Buffalo in 2004, and is now an Assistant Professor of Literacy at Le Moyne College, where he teaches Principles and Methods of Literacy Learning, Multicultural Literacy for Urban Education, and Adapting Literacy Learning for Students with Special Needs in both elementary and secondary programs. Originally from China, Dr. Ma taught for more than 10 years at both public school and university levels in a Chinese educational context. Currently he lives with his wife and daughter in Fayetteville, New York.

Being a cultural product of Chinese and North American education, Dr. Ma believes his cross-cultural experience and scholarship have provided him with a deep love and respect for teaching and conducting research related to culturally and linguistically diverse learners.

In addition to examining the theory, research, and practice about diverse learners' literacy development in a variety of sociocultural contexts, he is interested in exploring the use of discussion as an instructional tool, and in the Confucian perspective on learning, which he thinks may contribute to a more inclusive social constructivist view of learning.

**CORWIN
PRESS**

The Corwin Press logo—a raven striding across an open book—represents the union of courage and learning. Corwin Press is committed to improving education for all learners by publishing books and other professional development resources for those serving the field of PreK–12 education. By providing practical, hands-on materials, Corwin Press continues to carry out the promise of its motto: **"Helping Educators Do Their Work Better."**

1

Classroom Community: Getting to Know Me, Myself, and Us

STRATEGY 1
Autobiography: All About Me

Autobiographies, assigned at the beginning of the school year, not only help the teacher know the student's family background, but also the likes and dislikes that motivate. Sharing portions of autobiographies within the classroom also stimulates students to get to know each other for the development of a classroom learning community. As a result, research strongly suggests that students benefit academically and socially in such a community (Garcia, 2002; Heath, 1983; Slavin, 1990; Schmidt , 2005). English Language Learner (ELL) students find this strategy particularly empowering (Cummins, 1986; Igoa, 1995). They may bring information to the classroom not found in texts as primary sources. This can inspire a greater depth of understanding and appreciation of the curriculum.

ELA Standard: 9

Beginning Learners—All About Me

1. One or two students are given brown grocery bags to take home and fill with their favorite things. Suggestions are family pictures, toys, clothing, or gifts from grandparents or other people they care about.

2. During the daily sharing time, the student takes one item at a time out of the bag and talks about it. The item may be passed around or put on a special table for the day.

3. After the sharing, the rest of the class may ask questions for the student to answer.

4. When the students finish questioning, they write about their classmate and make a picture about him or her. These writings and drawings are shared throughout the day.

5. At the end of the day, the student takes home the class's written records in the form of a book with a cover designed by one of the classmates.

Intermediate Learners—Life Timeline

1. Students are given a roll of paper to create a timeline of their life stories.

2. They place significant remembered events along the line.

3. They may draw pictures or add snapshots of the events.

4. The may add a measurement line (like an EKG) along the timeline that depicts the highs and lows of their 12 years. A dip occurs with the loss of a grandparent. A peak occurs when given the first cat or dog.

5. Hang the timelines around the room.

6. Each person gets to tell his or her story.

Advanced Learners

1. Students write their autobiographies, starting from their earliest memories.

2. Students include family history, education, religion, holidays, celebrations, travels, pets, friends, victories, and defeats.

3. Students may want to share a special family artifact, like a military uniform, pottery, jewelry, toy, quilt, or recipe.

4. Students compare and contrast their stories with the biographies of famous people from several ethnic, cultural, and linguistic groups. Web sites of these famous people can inspire more research and a greater depth of understanding.

5. Discuss the biographies and explain what is admired about the people's lives.

Curriculum Connections

This strategy lends itself to any language arts or social studies program for beginning, intermediate, and advanced learners, at the start of the school year. From the beginning of class course work, students can situate themselves in specific eras studied during history and literature classes. Beginners start to think of themselves as part of a community. This relates to the study of community helpers. Intermediate learners study other nations and cultures within the United States as well as around the world. For advanced learners, who have the opportunity to be involved in social studies and English interdisciplinary thematic units, the autobiography is especially powerful. Autobiographies serve as a means for comparing and contrasting the past, present, and future with historical and literary periods.

Teachers' Comments

"Students like to talk or write about their favorite topics, themselves, and their communities. Even students with difficult family histories show pride in their discussions."

"What might seem unmentionable to us may be spoken or written without fear if the classroom is safe."

"Knowledge gained . . . places greater responssibility on the teacher, but gives a deeper understanding for working with students."

STRATEGY 2
Biography: What Do You Like?

Interviewing classmates to discover what they like at the beginning and throughout the school year would help students get to know each other and start an appreciation of each other. Television has provided many models for interviews, so students enjoy trying this themselves. The interview process also acts as a means to promote inquiry learning, where students are active classroom participants who connect with their learning environment and formulate questions (Chaille & Britain, 1991; Slavin, 1990). After the interview, using multicultural crayons, magic markers, paint, or other art forms, students may draw or color the persons interviewed, showing the individuals enjoying what they like. The pair helps each other throughout the process. Questions might include asking about favorite foods, television shows, music, games, people, places, holidays, or academics. Actually, students are not only learning about others but also participating in a form of character education related to compassion and empathy, higher-order processes (Berkowitz, 1998).

ELA Standard: 9

Beginning Learners

1. The teacher models the activity by selecting a student and asking the student what he or she likes. The teacher then writes a sentence and draws a simple picture showing one activity or thing the student enjoys.

2. Next, the students are paired and the students ask each other about the things they like.

3. Together, they select what to draw.

4. Then students may write/dictate a sentence about the person to be placed under the drawing.

5. Students may introduce their buddies and read the sentences and talk about the pictures.

Intermediate Learners

1. The teacher explains the interview process and models it with students.

2. Students and teacher create interview questions. Examples follow:
   - What foods do you like? Why?
   - What places do you like to go? Why?
   - Who are your favorite people? Why?
   - What is your favorite television show? Why?
   - What is your favorite thing? Why?
   - What is your favorite game? Why?
   - What is your favorite part of the school day? Why?

3. Students interview their partners and write the information.

4. Students draw pictures of their partners enjoying their favorite things, using multicultural crayons, paints, or magic markers.

5. Students write a paragraph about their partners.

6. Pictures and paragraphs are placed on a bulletin board, either inside or outside the classroom.

7. Time may be taken to read and discuss each person.

Advanced Learners

1. The teacher may model the interview process: What does a good interviewer do? What does the interviewee do? Lead a discussion concerning the importance of listening carefully to the person and writing what he or she says is important. The teacher can demonstrate by interviewing a person in the class, such as a teaching assistant, principal, parent, another teacher, or a special guest from the community.

2. Class discusses appropriate interview questions and composes a lengthy list of about 10 or more questions concerning "likes." Students are paired for interviews and the process begins, allowing for about 5 to 10 minutes for each interview depending on the size of the class.

3. Using multicultural media, such as magazines, students create a poster (2" × 3") of the person interviewed. Drawings, photos, etc. may be used to celebrate the person interviewed. Students work in pairs throughout the process.

4. Then the "likes" biography is written/typed and placed under the poster. Class discussion of each poster follows.

Curriculum Connections

This language arts or social studies activity includes reading, writing, listening, speaking, and viewing. Students will be able to monitor their own stories as well as be a special person among other special people. This is a positive way to build classroom learning communities where people actually know a lot about each other and are presented in a positive light. Of course, students may want to categorize the likes of certain people, showing how we are similar and different in our likes.

Teachers' Comments

"ELL students like this opportunity to share. Their parents sometimes join them."

"This is a nice way to get students to know each other. They've seen interviewing on television, and pretend to be Oprah or some other famous person."

"This strategy can be completed by all students, no matter what their learning differences, and they like it."

STRATEGY 3
Physical Differences

By age three, children notice human differences and actually realize what is most acceptable in society. Numerous studies have shown that children are well aware that being from European American or the white culture in the United States gives one a better chance (Barrera, 1992; Jensen, 2005; Tatum, 1992). Therefore, the appreciation of different perspectives and different physical appearances is important to emphasize in the classroom where reading, writing, listening, speaking, and viewing are developed (Schmidt, 1998a).

This strategy focuses on the physical dimensions of diversity among people. Making the noticeable differences in height, skin tone, and hair and eye colors explicit to students, they may come to be more consciously aware of the great diversity existing among their peers and in U.S. society at large. Although some may be initially uncomfortable talking about physical differences, open and explorative discussions by the students, with the teacher's guidance, may help the young minds to accept themselves and to accept each other as they are. Accepting attitudes as such may help students' social and emotional development. While implementing this strategy, the teacher needs to guide the students to be sensitive to others' feelings.

ELA Standard: 12

Beginning Learners

1. The teacher may begin by showing a picture of the Houston Rockets star Yao Ming and ask the students to guess his height (7 feet, 6 inches). The teacher may then use a yardstick to indicate how high 7 feet, 6 inches is on the wall, then invites volunteers to tell their height (or to measure their height using the yardstick) so as to show how much shorter the volunteers are in comparison to Yao Ming.

2. The teacher explains that people differ not only in height, but also in skin tone, hair, and eye colors.

3. The teacher asks the students to look around at each other and tell all the different hair colors they can find or think of, and the teacher will write down all the color words. For example, *auburn, blond(e), black, brown, brunette, chestnut, golden, grey, red-haired, sandy,* etc.

4. The teacher then asks the students to tell the skin colors they can find or think of. Again, the teacher will write down all the words for skin tone. For example, *albino, black, dark, fair, freckled, light, olive, pale, tan, white, yellow,* etc.

5. Similarly, the teacher asks the students to come up with words for eye colors, which the teacher writes down on the board. For example, *black, blue, brown, gray, green, hazel,* etc.

6. The teacher then explains that, although people have all these different physical features, we can still work together and become friends.

7. Finally, each student shakes hands with other classmates and says, "Let's be friends."

Intermediate Learners

1. Repeat Steps 1–7.

2. The teacher adds that the different races living in the U.S. tend to have different physical characteristics. For example, people of European backgrounds often have pale skin tones and a variety of hair and eye colors, whereas people of African backgrounds tend to have black or dark skin, hair, and eyes, whereas many Asian people have tan or light brown skin, and black eyes and hair.

3. Each student draws a portrait of him- or herself and shares the portrait with other students.

Advanced Learners

1. Repeat the above Steps 1 and 3.

2. The teacher explains that people's height and eye, hair, and skin colors are determined by the genes we inherit from our parents when we are born. (The teacher may add that, when they enter high school, the students will study more about genes in their biology class.) Therefore, it is normal to have this or that physical characteristic, because we are all different individuals.

3. Explain that, in spite of these physical differences, we still can and need to get along and work together as a learning community and as contributing citizens in the society.

4. Class will gather data about class physical differences and graph the results.

Curriculum Connections

This strategy may be used in social studies class, especially when topics related to cross-cultural relationships and conflicts are dealt with. In art class, the students may draw a colorful portrait to express their unique appearances. In addition, ELA teachers may use this strategy to encourage all students (especially students with physical disabilities or from diverse backgrounds) to feel comfortable about their physical appearances through descriptive discussions about all the physical differences. To facilitate students' writing development, the teacher may ask students to write an essay to describe their (another person's) appearance, adding vivid details and using other forms of expressions or writing devices (e.g., figures of speech) they have learned. Finally, the graphing experience relates to mathematics.

STRATEGY 4
Abilities and Capabilities

This strategy moves from considering the differences in physical dimensions to exploring differences in people's abilities and capabilities (cf. Strategy 3). As Gardner's (1999) work suggested, people have multiple intelligences. Therefore, open and explorative discussions of different ways of knowing the world and expressing themselves may help the young students to recognize their own special skills and talents, and to better understand their strengths and weaknesses. Examining diverse abilities and capabilities may also help students' cognitive, social, and affective development. Teachers who have students with low self-esteem may need to plan ahead. They should be prepared to address the talents of individual students.

ELA Standard: 12

Beginning and Intermediate Learners

1. The teacher may begin by explaining that people may be good at learning and doing different things, such as reading, writing, listening, speaking, mathematical calculations, drawing, coloring, athletics, music, interacting with other people, thinking, and self-reflection.

2. The teacher may share what he or she is good at with the students. For example, the teacher may be good at writing poems, singing songs, playing a musical instrument, speaking a foreign language, playing basketball, etc.

3. The teacher explains to the students that they may have some skills or talents that are special and meaningful, but may not have been realized by themselves or others.

4. The teacher brainstorms with students about their interests. If there are English as a Second Language (ESL) learners in the class, the teacher may encourage them to share a few words in their first language. The teacher writes what the students think are their abilities and capabilities.

5. The teacher explains (after identifying some students' strengths in the class) that people may have different abilities and capabilities, just as they may have different physical differences. For example, John may be skilled in using words to express his feelings and thoughts, Kate may be good at playing violin, Lucy may be strong at drawing, and Matt may be quick at solving math problems. It is perfectly fine (and natural) if any of them has skills or talents different from those of someone else. It is most useful to find out what one's genuine interests and abilities are in order to further develop them and make them even stronger.

Advanced Learners

1. Repeat Steps 1–5.

2. The teacher may provide the students opportunities to display their special skills or talents by writing a poem, drawing a picture, singing

a song, speaking a foreign language, playing a musical instrument, creating artwork, or doing whatever skill they are capable.

3. Based on the results of the above step, the teacher may organize a talent show by the students.

Curriculum Connections

This strategy may be used across the curriculum. In ELA class, the teacher may ask students to write an essay on what they think about the multiple ways of sense-making and problem solving and to celebrate the various abilities among them. In social studies class, the teacher may use the strategy to highlight the importance of recognizing people's abilities and at the same time of working with others of various abilities at school and in the society at large. In math class, the teacher may give students easy but tricky questions to promote their mathematical thinking and learning (cf. Strategy 24).

STRATEGY 5
Graphing Different Ethnic Groups in the U.S.

Central to this strategy is an awareness of the diverse peoples living and working in the United States and calling this land their country. Providing opportunities for students to search for the number of people from different ethnic backgrounds and to document the figures, using a variety of visual tools, helps to cultivate in the young learners a keener awareness of the diversity among the U.S. population (www.census.gov). Such an awareness contributes to a more accepting class/school culture, and is congruent with the societal goal of ethnic and racial tolerance and respect for a more harmonious multicultural society.

ELA Standards: 8 and 12

Beginning Learners

1. The teacher may begin by showing the U.S. Population Clock, explaining that in the United States there is one birth every 8 seconds. (The teacher may ask the students to all be quiet for 8 seconds, saying "This is how long it takes another baby to be born in the U.S."). One international migrant comes to the U.S. every 26 seconds, and the U.S. has a gain of one person every 13 seconds.

2. The teacher explains that the U.S. population is made of people from many racial backgrounds and geographical regions. For example, there are people originating from Europe, Africa, and Asia, as well as Native Americans. That is part of the reason why the U.S. has been known as "a nation of nations."

3. The teacher explains that all students should be able to accept work and play with the other students in the class.

Intermediate Learners

1. Repeat Steps 1–3.

2. The teacher adds that, according to U.S. Census 2000 data, the U.S. population was 281,421,906, of which Whites made up about 62.6 percent, Hispanics or Latinos about 12.5 percent, African Americans about 12.3 percent, Asians 3.6 percent, American Indians and Alaska Natives about 0.9 percent, Native Hawaiians and other Pacific Islanders about 0.1 percent, and other races about 5.5 percent. (These figures were based on the U.S. census data and the authors' research.)

3. The teacher helps the students use Excel to create a bar or pie chart to represent the numbers obtained from the U.S. population data.

Racial Distribution of U.S. Population

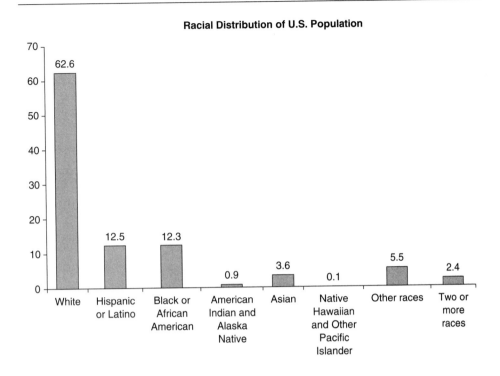

Racial Distribution of U.S. Population

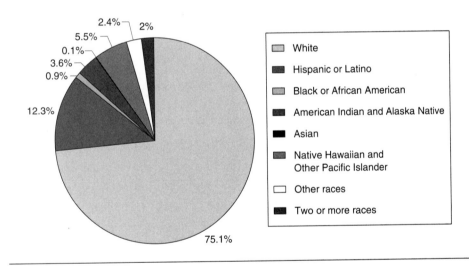

Advanced Learners

1. Repeat the above Steps 1–3.

2. The teacher divides the class into groups of four students for more detailed research. For example, the teacher asks the students to break down some of the big categories such as *Asian* into smaller categories such as *Asian Indian, Chinese, Filipino, Japanese, Korean, Vietnamese,* and *Other Asian.* The students then search for the specific numbers and percentages of the people for the smaller categories. The results are summarized below.

Asian U.S. Population	10,242,998	3.6%
Asian Indian	1,678,765	0.6%
Chinese	2,432,585	0.9%
Filipino	1,850,314	0.7%
Japanese	796,700	0.3%
Korean	1,076,872	0.4%
Vietnamese	1,122,528	0.4%
Other Asian	1,285,234	0.5%

3. Each group then uses a bar chart to visually represent their findings, as illustrated below.

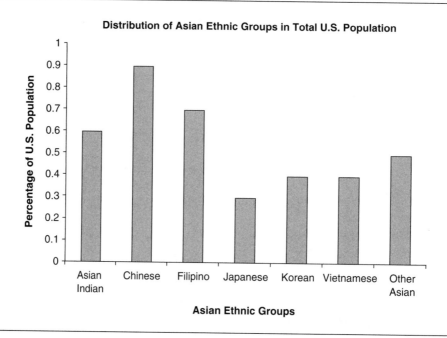

Distribution of Asian Ethnic Groups in Total U.S. Population

4. Similarly, students could create bar or pie charts about the distribution of Hispanics or Latinos in total U.S. population or the Hispanics in the U.S. by origin, shown below.

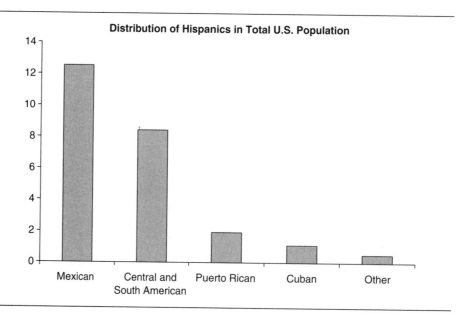

Distribution of Hispanics in Total U.S. Population

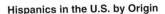

Hispanics in the U.S. by Origin

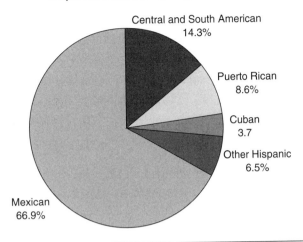

Curriculum Connections

This strategy can be used in the social studies or math classes. Through searching for and graphing the numbers of people in the U.S. population from varied racial backgrounds, students may develop a clearer understanding of the diversity in the U.S. population and in U.S. society. Learning how to use the bar and pie charts to visually represent the numbers may also help students use these visual organizers for math problems and for reading and writing informational texts. Moreover, the teacher may ask students to write an essay on what they have learned about racial and ethnic diversity.

STRATEGY 6
Graphing Differences for Analysis

This strategy aims at introducing techniques for graphing information about various forms of diversity among people. For example, the teacher may use this strategy for students to make comparisons with one another, or between characters in books or across content learned over time. The interpersonal comparison not only helps to promote a deeper understanding of the differences and similarities among students, but also involves useful skills for synthesizing informational texts. The following steps focus on making comparisons and contrasts to showcase how the strategy may be applied for different purposes.

ELA Standards: 8 and 12

Beginning Learners

1. The teacher facilitates each student to create a personal profile. Each student lists his or her physical characteristics (height, hair and eye colors, and so on), age, schooling, special talents, personal interests, etc.

2. Each student talks to a good friend or a classmate to obtain similar information about that individual's profile.

3. The students fold a page top-down in the middle. On the left-hand side, each student enters the things gathered from Step 1; on the right-hand side of the page, enters the things gathered from Step 2. The students may draw pictures or use symbols to illustrate their ideas instead of writing everything in words.

4. The teacher divides the class into groups of four, and each student takes turns sharing the results with other members.

5. After group sharing, the teacher wraps up by explaining to the students that it is nice to be different and that diversity is normal.

Intermediate Learners

1. Repeat Steps 1–5.

2. The teacher explains to the students that there are different types of computer software (e.g., Microsoft Word) that may be used to make visual organizers for comparison and contrast. The teacher demonstrates to each group about how to use Word to make a contrast table or a Venn diagram, as illustrated below.

3. Each group works on the computer to graph a contrast table or a Venn diagram and to enter the accompanying text for comparison.

Advanced Learners

1. Repeat the above Steps 1–3.

2. The teacher asks the students to choose two characters from a novel they have recently read, and use either a Venn diagram or a contrast table to highlight their differences and similarities.

Table 1.1   Contrast Table

My profile	My friend's profile
1.	1.
2.	2.
3.	3.
4.	4.
5.	5.

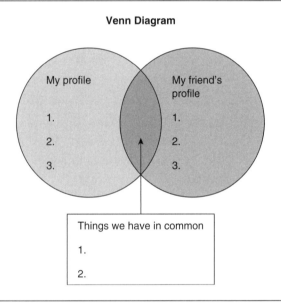

Venn Diagram

My profile
1.
2.
3.

My friend's profile
1.
2.
3.

Things we have in common
1.
2.

3. Based on the information, the students write a short essay to explain and interpret the results.

Curriculum Connections

This strategy may be used in math class. While the beginning learners may just hand-draw charts to compare and visually present their ideas about who they are and who a friend is, the intermediate and advanced students will learn to use word processing software to make a Venn diagram or contrast table for such an analysis. The hands-on experience of using the computer to make visual representations of textual information may also help their development of computer literacy. In addition, the skills to use visual organizers such as a Venn diagram or contrast table to synthesize informational texts are useful in ELA and social studies as well, as shown in the above steps with the advanced learners.

STRATEGY 7
What's in a Name?

The sweetest thing a person hears is his or her own name. Names reveal family cultural identity, family ideas, ideals, and/or histories. Students at all ages enjoy activities around their names. Studying names at all grade levels reveals human similarities and differences and assists the teacher in developing culturally responsive lessons starting with student names. ELL students will be helped by the teacher or a study buddy to complete the activity. This is actually a way to learn English adjectives (Igoa, 1995). A kindergarten child from India who was learning English enjoyed making ornate designs of flowers around his name. His was very different from the other children's and was greatly appreciated for its beauty (Schmidt, 1998a).

ELA Standard: 6

Beginning Learners

In the early grades, learning to write the entire name is an important accomplishment. Students may learn to write their names in large letters in the middle of a 9" × 12" sheet of unlined paper. Then they may decorate around the name, with crayons or other media, showing pictures of what they like to do. They can then share their pictures with the class. The teacher may pin up the name creations and send home notes asking family members to tell the students about their names. The following is an example of a survey to be sent home to families.

MY NAME IS SWEET TO HEAR

We are studying the names of the students in our classroom to help them see and appreciate differences and similarities. Please complete this survey and talk about it with your student tonight. Then send it to school with your student. Thank you so much for helping us show our students how important they are!

Who named your student?

Why was your student given that name?

If your student was named after a close friend or someone in your family, would that person come to visit our classroom?

Adjectives	Verbs
Jacquil Keevers	
J Jubilant	Jumps
A Anxious	Acts
C Cute	Cleans
Q Quick	Quivers
U Understanding	Understands
I Intelligent	Inquires
L Lively	Likes
K Knowledgeable	Knows
E Exciting	Energizes
E Extraordinary	Explains
V Vital	Values
E Enviable	Enlivens
R Raucous	Reads
S Studious	Studies

Intermediate Learners

1. Students write their complete names, and then in pairs, they help each other associate adjectives describing each other with each letter of the name. Pairs change, and then complete names are written again, associating verbs that describe each other with each letter of the name.

2. Now, have students write a sentence using each adjective and verb that describes Jacquil and talks about the way he behaves.

3. Homework: Have students find out who named them and why they were given that name.

Advanced Learners

1. Have students complete the above activity and homework. Then research their name. Have them find out as much information as possible concerning their complete name. Ask them to discover the origins of their name, historically and linguistically. For example, Irene comes from a word meaning "serenity." Patricia or Patrick comes from a word meaning "aristocrat."

Curriculum Connections

Students in the earliest grades are learning to write their own names. There is research that supports the idea that learning to write your name before school actually assists in literacy development (Morris, Bloodgood, & Perney, 2003). Students learn that their name is a group of symbols that create a word. In later grades, adjectives and verbs can be associated with personal characteristics and assigned to various names providing a grammar lesson. Finally, researching the historical origins of a name provides a means for studying culture, language, and history. For example, Smith and Schmidt were names given to those who were blacksmiths, in England and Germany, respectively.

Teachers' Comments

"There is no doubt in my mind that this strategy inspires all students to think about adjectives and remember what they are."

"Students love talking about themselves, and their names give them permission to do just that."

"It is the simplest way to get everyone involved and begin to get students thinking about who they are and where their countries of origin might be. I think it helps develop an understanding of our great country."

STRATEGY 8
A Web Page: An Electronic Book About You

This strategy combines print literacy with multimedia literacy. Each student will create his or her own Web page using words and multiple forms of expression, including (but not limited to) pictures, design, and music. In some ways, it is almost like making an interactive electronic book about oneself. At the end of the class project, students may combine their work into one volume or post them on a safe online site. In addition, this strategy may be adapted for other computer-based learning activities, such as for students to explore a variety of topics on the Internet, which are presented in the last section of this book. Important: teachers need to be cautious about possible risks involved in students using the Internet. We suggest strongly that, before students post their personal Web pages online, teachers learn the school policy regarding online access and use, and school-approved safe sites for students (cf. Strategy 46).

ELA Standards: 8 and 12

Beginning Learners

1. The teacher helps the students brainstorm ideas about themselves, such as name, age, pets, hobbies, etc. Then each student enters his or her information on the computer.

2. As most beginning learners have not yet grasped the needed literacy skills, they may use some common icons or symbols instead of complete sentences to express their ideas.

3. The teacher may need to work one-on-one with some students who are less proficient in using the computer to complete their Web pages. In general, different levels of sophistication should be allowed for different students' Web pages.

Intermediate Learners

1. To get students started, the teacher may ask each student to write short paragraphs about some of the categories to be included on the Web page, such as *My Favorite Sports, Foods, Books,* or *Music.*

2. Each student may also be asked to write a brief account about his or her personal characteristics, such as nickname, age, gender, height, hair and eye color, etc.

3. While working on their Web pages, they can make use of these sources of information in their creation. Additionally, they may form study groups to discuss issues or problems related to wording different categories or using different designs.

Advanced Learners

1. The teacher and the whole class brainstorm categories to be included on the Web page. Possible categories may include pseudonym, age, personal characteristics, school, city, talents, favorite sports/foods/books/music, best friends, favorite school subjects, hobbies, interests, etc.

2. Based on the results of class discussions, the teacher prepares a worksheet that includes all these categories. The teacher explains that each student may write down the relevant information under each category to be entered on the Web page, but he or she may include additional information about himself or herself.

3. The students will enter the relevant information using hypertext markup language (HTML), Publisher, or PowerPoint. It is important for the teacher to encourage the students to be creative. For example, the student may use online communication icons, scan and insert pictures, add music, make use of color backgrounds or different fonts, or use pop-ups for interactive or special effects. In addition, students may be encouraged to write long and rich accounts about some of the categories.

4. Each student will have an opportunity to present his or her Web page to the whole class using a projector. Students may provide feedback on each other's creations for sharing and for revision.

5. After presentation and revision, the teacher may ask the students to print out their work and put them into one volume as a class project. The teacher may also help the students post their Web pages on a school-approved, password-protected site.

Curriculum Connections

This strategy combines reading and writing with computer-based media literacy. Through these multiple forms of hands-on literacy experiences, students are provided with opportunities to think about who they are and what they like, thus helping them to learn literacy, as well as get a better understanding of their developing identity.

STRATEGY 9
ABC's of Communication:
Getting to Know You in a Few Minutes

This strategy helps to build classroom community from the beginning of the school year. It can be completed in about 5 to 10 minutes. There are four steps that can be completed in small groups and pairs on a daily basis until all students have personally shared with each other. Similarities and differences can be celebrated every day. Students at all levels benefit from this strategy. This strategy is based on the model known as the ABC's *of Cultural Understanding and Communication* (Schmidt, 1998b ; 2000; 2001; 2005). Those who experience the model's process write in-depth autobiographies (Banks, 1994), interview those who are culturally different (Schmidt, 2000; Xu, 2000), complete cross-cultural analyses (Finkbeiner & Koplin, 2002) and design home/school/community connections, and create culturally relevant lesson plans (Schmidt, 1999b, 2005). The major premise of the model is the adage, "Know thyself and understand others."

ELA Standard: 5

Beginning Learners

1. Early learners may choose to talk about something they like or some event that has happened with a classmate, while practicing listening, sharing, and reporting to the whole group. The teacher may record similarities and differences each day. The class may read them together and then write their own.

Intermediate Learners

1. **Autobiography**—Have students close their eyes and think about their earliest memories that have to do with family, education, religion, happy times, anything that they remember that they can share with another person-1 minute.
2. **Biography**—One person shares his or her own memories for a minute while the other listens. Then the listener shares for a minute.
3. **Compare and Contrast**—Sharing partners or groups talk about similarities and differences in life experiences.
4. **Describe this brief experience to the rest of the group in a word or a phrase.** Each student shares a word or phrase, like "fun" or "interesting" to sum up related experiences or "new ideas about playing" to describe new learning about each other that came from sharing.

Advanced Learners

1. Students write their autobiographies, including as many memories as possible about many aspects in their lives—family, celebrations, pets, school, victories. (Teacher models with his or her own life experiences.)

2. Students pair up for the interview process—questions to ask are created by the class to ensure that they will not be too personal.

3. Students then fill in Venn diagrams or charts that compare and contract similarities and differences.

4. Next, students write compare-and-contrast paragraphs regarding themselves and their partners.

5. Finally, students share these writings in class and throughout the school year whenever there are discussions concerning point of view and perspectives.

Curriculum Connections

The ABC's activity can be used periodically throughout the school year in any class to discuss differences in perspectives and backgrounds. This helps students become aware of similarities and differences and develop an appreciation of differences in all aspects of people and learning. This is especially helpful when dealing with inquiry learning in science and mathematics, with perspectives on major historical events, and with reader response when interpreting literature.

Teachers' Comments

"Teaching students to look at other perspectives can be challenging, but this model seems to help them get started."

"What makes the ABC's so good to use in the classroom is that you can adapt it easily."

"There is something about the ABC's that helps the students quickly see similarities and differences easily. They wrote great compare-and-contrast paragraphs."

Home, Community, and Nation: Making Contributions to Literacy Learning

STRATEGY 10
What Is a Family?

The purpose of this strategy is to assist students in defining the human family on many different levels. (As a class, family may be defined as adults who care for you. Students may then speak of aunts, uncles, sisters, brothers, teachers, church members, and/or shelter friends as family.) Students in high-poverty areas often see their church families, their neighbors, and distant cousins as family. They rely on family-type relationships to survive on a daily basis (Payne, DeVol, & Smith, 2005). The students study their own families and those of others in the classroom, state, nation, and world, and begin to see that families can be different. This helps them see that they are part of a wider community, a community that should care and share and show responsibility for one another (Schmidt, 2005; Schmidt & Pailliotet, 2001).

ELA Standard: 12

Beginning Learners

1. Have Students bring family pictures to school or draw family pictures. Class magazines may also contain pictures of people who might look

like family members. These can be cut out and pasted on a sheet and presented as what student's families look like.

2. Students talk about family by discussing what they do with their family daily, on weekends, at holidays, etc.

3. Students draw or paint a picture of what they like to do with their family.

4. Students talk about who helps them learn about the world in their family.

5. Students talk about learning at home, and take home a disposable camera to photograph people and things that help them learn at home. For example, "Grandma reads to me, television tells me new stuff, computer games help me read." Teacher or family develops photos. Students share with the class. A collage is created and taken home.

6. Students invite a family member into the class to share in the study of classroom families and talk about the responsibilities of each family member.

7. Students make a list of their responsibilities in the family.

8. Using youth literature, briefly study different families and communities in your area, nation, and world.

9. The class writes a definition of family and what it means to be a part of a family. The definition is the title of a bulletin board display of the class's families intermingled with photos and drawings. Below is a possible idea.

FAMILY IS A GROUP OF PEOPLE WHO CARE AND SHARE WITH EACH OTHER

Somebody makes dinner
Somebody cleans our home
Somebody goes to a job
Somebody learns
Somebody teaches
Somebody plays
Somebody hugs
Somebody washes
Somebody takes care of clothes
Somebody feeds our pet
Somebody takes care of the yard
Somebody takes care of me
Somebody takes care of the baby

Intermediate Learners

1. Students bring family pictures to school.

2. Students write about their families, including family member responsibilities.

3. Each student receives a disposable camera to record evidence of learning at home.

4. Pictures are developed by family or teacher and discussed to show how people learn at home.

5. Each student invites a family member to a classroom learning/ teaching discussion. Students present their learning/teaching at-home experiences.

6. The teacher reinforces learning/teaching at home. Family members share something special about their families—a song, a story, or an object.

7. Study families from around the world, using the Internet, literature, and visitors.

8. Study other families who live in our state and nation—Northeast, Southwest, Northwest, Central, and so on—using the Internet and literature.

9. Study community family differences and similarities and invite local family members who are Native American or new to this country and ask them to share something with the class, such as a dance, a song, a piece of art, a special story.

Advanced Learners

1. Study family structure from the past to the present in American history. The following are examples of possible study questions: What influences guided family structure? What guided family structure in farming communities, in mountain communities, in seacoast communities, in manufacturing communities? Analyze division of labor, religion, and social norms.

2. Study Native American family structures. The Iroquois in New York State were matriarchal.

3. Research family heritage using family interviews and Internet resources to discover family history. Invite family and community members into the classroom to expand on the interviews.

4. Create a class play with costumes and scenery that demonstrate family structures from Colonial times to the present day. Write a play that includes several vignettes in each era. Students may want to use actual family names. For example: The Smiths came over on the Mayflower . . . the Briattis, who came over on a boat in 1900 from Italy . . . the Norstoms, who came from Sweden and decided to head west in a covered wagon.

5. Present the play during the school day to the entire school. Present in the evening for the community.

Curriculum Connections

History, art, and language arts are perfect connections for these strategies. Students will have firsthand opportunities to draw, write, interview, and research. Visitors are important at all learning levels, and active involvement and cultural relevancy are clearly present when using this strategy.

Teachers' Comments

"This is a way to know the families of your kids. It's real."

"I began to understand my children with this strategy."

"Students are generally proud of who they call family. This gets them to talk, read, and write."

STRATEGY 11
Home Is Where the Heart Is:
Connecting With Families

The purpose of this strategy is to encourage students to bring meaningful items from home to present and share with the class. The classmates will get to know each other, and the teacher will gain knowledge of students' families and interests. Students will have opportunities to talk about something familiar and allow classmates to ask questions. Additionally, students will be able to practice decoding, spelling, and composing (Watson & Ecken, 2003).

ELA Standard: 11

Beginning Learners

1. Students will be asked to bring objects that remind them of their homes. These may be photos, or personal items such as toys or clothing. The item may be brought in by a parent if necessary, and could include a family book, a clock, a game, a favorite food item, or anything that makes the student think of home.

2. These are shared during a morning meeting of students, giving students an opportunity to tell about the items and explain why they remind them of their families.

3. Students in the class may ask three or four questions after the item is explained.

4. The class can then list the items on a chart with classmates' names next to them.

5. This will allow students to practice pronouncing the names of the items throughout the week. It may become a center during language arts. Two students could practice the words, taking turns being teacher and student.

Intermediate Learners

1. Follow steps 1–4.

2. Allow students to write a short story using two or more of the people and their objects. They may also illustrate the story.

3. The stories are shared during the following week with the whole class.

4. A class book may be created from the stories.

Advanced Learners

1. Follow steps 1–3.

2. Students take notes about each object.

3. Students in pairs categorize and analyze the information collected.

4. Students write about the experience and share their interpretations and conclusions concerning the class.

5. Students may decide to place these objects on display in the classroom, thus bringing their investments to the setting. (Precautions need to be taken concerning any damage to property, so a special shelf may need to be used for display items.)

Curriculum Connections

Decoding, spelling, and composing will be practiced for language arts learning. Also, students will need to collect and analyze data to make interpretations concerning the class.

Teachers' Comments

"When they bring objects from home and leave them in the classroom, they take ownership of the room."

"Where the object is placed is almost like a homestead. They stake out a claim in the classroom."

"They learn to respect others' property. They learn to trust their classmates."

STRATEGY 12
Community Soup

This strategy helps students see what their community has to offer and how it relates to their school learning (Edwards, 2004). Students will visit places in their community, and people from the places will visit the classroom. If students cannot go on a neighborhood walk or bus trip, the people involved can visit the classroom, bringing pictures of their establishments with key information. A farmer may bring pictures of his farm and a tool that he uses at the farm. A florist may bring pictures from the shop with sample flowers and decorations used for arrangements. The first time the teachers in urban settings did this, they realized it was time-consuming, but the results of the project were so positive that they have continued.

ELA Standard: 7

Beginning Learners

Students begin an in-depth study of immediate neighborhoods: rural might be the local farm and village people; urban might include neighborhood shops, fire station, and recreation center; suburban might include housing developments and local town shops.

1. An enlarged map is made of the local community and spread on the floor or desks, with the main streets and roads and locations of homes. Digital pictures may be taken of homes, shops, and significant landmarks.

2. Students paste digital pictures on the map and label. Students study the compass and plot their trip on the map.

3. The students then take a field trip visiting the local establishments near the school. A fish store, pizza shop, Chinese restaurant, gas station, hair salon, drugstore, laundry, and daycare center might be on the list. At each site, the proprietors contribute to community soup with a can of vegetables or broth given to them the day before by the teacher. The proprietor or worker briefly tells about the business and what it does for the neighborhood.

4. Students return to the school to write thank-you notes and invitations to the Community Soup Luncheon held in their classroom. These are sent.

5. The following week, students survey the ingredients and chart the recipe. Parents are invited to make and serve the soup using the school cafeteria.

6. The students write alphabet poems about the community helpers they have studied and the shops visited. Each student reads a poem at the luncheon. Each guest receives a place mat decorated for their shop. The

soup is cooked in the cafeteria and served in the kindergarten room by parents of the students.

Intermediate Learners

1. Students and teacher list community resources found around the school.

2. On enlarged map placed on the wall, students name streets and roads and locate community spots, as well as their own homes. They may draw or bring in photos of their homes or places.

3. Directionality and the science and history of magnetism can be integrated as students use and study the compass.

4. Interview questions may be designed by the class in preparation for visits.

5. Students might request from each community person what ingredient would be a great addition to the soup. These could be contributed by the community person, if he or she volunteers, or by the students.

6. Students send out invitations for the Community Soup Luncheon and chart the ingredients contributed and what is needed to complete the recipe.

7. Students, in pairs, are responsible for creating an advertisement for each place visited. The advertisements are presented on the day of the luncheon.

8. Parents and students create the soup in the school cafeteria and serve the soup to the community visitors.

Advanced Learners

1. Students may study the local community and research what businesses can be called upon.

2. Students may decide on a luncheon menu and ask businesses to donate recipe items for the luncheon. They may send a letter describing the project, along with an invitation to the luncheon.

3. Students follow up with a phone call or visit to each business.

4. Students videotape skits/ads for the community businesses.

5. On the day of the luncheon, students make and serve the lunch with family and cafeteria volunteers.

6. On the day of the luncheon, students present the videotapes representing the businesses.

7. Students write and send thank-you notes to the businesses.

Curriculum Connections

Language arts, mathematics, art, science, and economics of the community are all part of understanding local and state history as it relates to national social studies. Through such themed instruction, students can learn about the relevance of all content areas to learning about their community. The language arts provide the tools that assist in learning as school and community work together to create relevancy that motivates teaching and learning.

Teachers' Comments

"It's time-consuming when you first try this strategy, but it's well worth the time. Volunteer support is amazing."

"This strategy suits so many different ways of practicing reading, writing, listening, speaking, and viewing."

"Students see possibilities for future careers. It opens eyes to what could be."

STRATEGY 13
Heroes and Sheroes: Contributions to Our World

This strategy offers students the opportunity to recognize heroes and sheroes in their midst. Loved ones are heroes who protect and care for them. They may be family members, teachers, friends, and neighbors. Local politicians, newscasters, and community helpers may all be included as they explore what it means to be a hero. Those people can be celebrated in the classroom as models of adult behavior (McGovern, 1997). Everyday heroes and sheroes are what make our lives good. Furthermore, study of everyday heroes and sheroes leads to analysis of national and international heroes.

ELA Standard: 1

Beginning Learners

1. Discuss heroes and sheroes in books, stories, and current events.

2. Read portions of *Seven Brave Women,* by Hearne (1997), a picture book for K–8. Discussions, drawing/painting/writing/sharing may occur.
   – Why is someone a hero or shero?
   – How can you be a hero or shero?

1. Tell family stories about family heroes or sheroes. For example, my brother saved a baby bird by putting it back into a nest. My mother works two jobs, so we can have a good life. My sister works with the volunteer firefighters.

2. Discussions, drawing, painting, writing, and sharing may occur.

3. Have a hero/shero party. Invite them to class and present pictures and words to each. Take photos with each student and his or her hero and/or shero. Place photos on bulletin board as a reminder.

Intermediate Learners

1. All of the above ideas are appropriate with additional activities.

2. Search the local newspaper to find human interest stories of local heroes and sheroes, such as someone giving back a wallet full of money, or someone saving a litter of puppies by the side of the road, or a student who called 911 when she noticed that Grandma wasn't breathing well.

3. Discuss the characteristics of a hero or shero.
   – Why do people become heroes?
   – Categorize heroes and sheroes.
   – Discuss whether you would want a hero or shero as a friend.
   – Create scripts and act out heroic situations . . . possibly some found in the newspaper or family heroic experiences.

– Have a celebration for family and community heroes and sheroes. Invite them to school and read what was written about them and act out a few of the scripts.

– For the school newspaper, report the celebration with pictures and a story.

Advanced Learners

1. All of the above.

2. In small groups or pairs, list past and present national and international heroes and sheroes—gather heroes and sheroes from every continent.

3. Study past and present national and international sheroes and heroes and their accomplishments.

4. Compare and contrast national and international heroes and sheroes with personal and local heroes and sheroes.

5. Each student selects a past or present national or international hero or shero and pretends to be that person by speaking on a particular national or international issue.

6. These could be videotaped and presented in other classrooms in the school.

Curriculum Connections

All content areas have everyday heroes: nurses, custodians, bus drivers, carpenters, mothers, fathers, relatives, and friends. For science, a bus driver may talk about safety issues related to bus mechanics, and a Wendy's worker may talk about proper food handling. For social studies, a newscaster may talk about reporting issues, and a friend or relative who is running for office can talk about being a patriot. A soldier may talk about his or her time in another country. A grocery worker may talk about knowing mathematics and how to make sure people get what they pay for.

Teachers' Comments

"We had a great turnout of local heroes and sheroes!"

"Students really got into trying to dress up like the hero and shero."

"Students performed a service for the school when they acted out famous heroes and sheroes. Several students went into other classrooms in the lower grades and had the children guess who they were."

STRATEGY 14
A Day in the Life of Youth/Adults

This strategy helps students see the similarities and differences among classmates and other youth in our world. It is a way of teaching our students to look beyond themselves to help them appreciate differences. Additionally, students are learning about others by first thinking of their own prior knowledge and experiences (Rumelhart, 1982). This makes learning relevant.

ELA Standard: 1

Beginning Learners

1. The teacher asks the whole class of students how their day begins and records responses on chart paper, on a white board, or a chalkboard.

2. Next, the teacher, with the students, records the typical school day. Discussion and rereading occurs throughout the process. (This is actually an LEA, or language experience approach—the teacher is recording students' comments, and students take turns reading the comments aloud while pointing to or framing each word, or the whole class rereads each statement as the teacher points to or frames words.

3. Then each student draws/writes about their day.

My Day

by
Ashley Littletree

I wake up.
I eat cereal.
I brush my teeth.
I get clothes for school.
I get my backpack.
I get the bus.
I go to school.
I play in the house center.
I go to library.
I go home.
I play with my dog.
I eat supper.
I watch TV.
My Mother reads to me.
I go to sleep.

Introduction	Similarities
Introduce the report (A few sentences)	Compare how we are alike (At least five sentences)
Differences	**Conclusions**
Contrast how we are different (At least five sentences)	What are you feeling or thinking? Why? (At least five sentences)

4. Teachers may make a laminated book for the class to share or a bulletin board display for compare-and-contrast similarities and differences discussions.

5. Students may individually present his or her day.

Intermediate Learners

1. The students describe food, clothing, shelter, family, and geography of their community.

2. Then the teacher or groups of students read Virginia Kroll's *Masai and I.*

3. From the reading, they create Venn diagrams showing similarities and differences between the Masai and themselves.

4. They then write four paragraphs concerning *Masai and I.* As a note-taking experience, they use the above format.

Advanced Learners

1. Each student records his or her typical day and shares with a small group of four or five people.

2. Each student may study an era in history to discover the lives of young people who lived in the U.S.A. 100 years ago or 200 years ago.

3. Relating to the social studies curriculum, each group is assigned to study a day in the life of a male or female student from a particular group of people in the United States or the world.

Figure 2.1   Masai and I

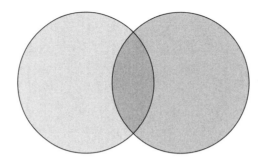

4. With the help of literature, the Internet, and interviews, students search for information about the typical day of a young person who is from a different culture or country, for example, Japanese, Mexican, farm family, city family, a family in Alaska or Hawaii, or new to this country.

5. If the school has new arrivals to the U.S.A., ask these students to talk about their daily lives in another country.

6. Students create a display for the school, depicting a day in the life of students around the world.

Curriculum Connections

Language arts and history are integrated as students read, write, listen, speak, and view information about the people in their communities and world. Students acquire the practice necessary for paragraph writing as they share their own lives and compare and contrast with others.

Teachers' Comments

"What better way to understand our place in the world than studying others and comparing and contrasting daily life."

"My little ones understand the similarities and differences in their classroom. This is a beginning for understanding different ways of seeing the world."

STRATEGY 15
Yesterday and Today: Grandparents/ Senior Citizens and Parents

The purpose of this strategy is to help students see the changes in the lives of family and country from one generation to another. Grandparents often have a special relationship with grandchildren, so their involvement in students' education can be powerful. Senior citizens enjoy being adopted as class grandparents, tutors, and school resources, so students who have no contact with grandparents may adopt a grandparent in their school (Payne, DeVol, & Smith, 2005). This strategy aims to bring family and community together and develop student pride and understanding of family and community.

ELA Standard: 7

Beginning Learners

1. Students talk about grandparents and bring pictures to school.

2. Students talk about what they do or did with grandparents.

3. Draw/write/paint about them and be ready to talk about the creations.

4. Have students invite one or both grandparents or parents to school to tell the class about their days in school. Have the grandparents talk about the parents' schools, too.

5. Share student creations on the day grandparents come to school.

Intermediate Learners

1. Begin with Steps 1 and 2 of the above.

2. Students interview grandparents to discover what school and growing up were like in their days. They ask questions about school, teachers, studies, work, friends, sports, games, music, etc.

3. Students interview parents to discover what school and growing up were like in their days. They ask questions about school, teachers, studies, work, friends, sports, games, music, etc.

4. Compare and contrast similarities and differences between parents and grandparents using charts or Venn diagrams.

5. Students write about the times they would prefer to live . . . Grandma's school days or Dad's school days? Students explain why and create a drawing, song, dance, costume, or poem that reflects the days they prefer.

6. Students invite parents or grandparents to school and perform the above activities for them.

Advanced Learners

1. Students bring in pictures of parents and grandparents to share in class.

2. Students share photos in small groups and tell what they know about their lives.

3. Students prepare interview questions about their lives and practice interviewing and taking notes in pairs. They ask questions about school, teachers, studies, work, friends, sports, games, music, etc.

4. First, students interview a grandparent or a person from the same generation. At the end of the interview, students ask if they would have preferred growing up in the student's generation. Students ask them to explain their answers.

5. Next, students interview a parent or a person from the same generation. At the end of the interview, studens ask if they would have preferred growing up in the student's generation. Students ask them to explain their answers.

6. Last, students write their own answers to the interview questions and also tell whether they would prefer to have grown up during the time of their grandparents or the time of their parents. They also must explain why.

7. Groups of students can collect and analyze the data or information. They can experiment with making charts that help to interpret the information gathered.

8. The class can then decide what they think the information means to them personally, to the local community, and to our nation.

9. Writing about all these discoveries may become a great article for the local newspaper.

Curriculum Connections

Reading, writing, listening, speaking, and viewing across the curriculum are in constant use during the implementation of this strategy. Mathematics is a key component for advanced learning, but simple graphing of characteristics from interviews could be included for the beginner and intermediate student. Additionally, the recent history of our country can be explored through primary sources, parents, and grandparents.

Teachers' Comments

"Our students bring friends and neighbors to school to share memories of our nation and local community. It makes history memorable."

"Students learn different perspectives on history not found in books."

"I always check to make sure my students have someone to ask. If they don't, we have people in our school and community members I know to ask for them."

STRATEGY 16
Place Name Games and Geographic Awareness

This strategy works as a competitive game. It engages groups of students in naming places around different themes in a number of ways. For example, themes may include oceans, continents, or countries in the world, or rivers, lakes, states/provinces, cities, or towns in a country. It may be used for practice or review of social studies or geography contents to help students remember geographic information or historical places covered in social studies or geography texts. It may also be used to increase students' awareness of geographical diversity.

ELA Standards: 11 and 12

Beginning Learners

1. The teacher first helps students form game groups, then assigns a "geographical theme" for each group, or students are allowed to decide on the theme. As beginning learners typically have not developed extensive geographical knowledge, the themes need to be more "local" and may include such names as their city, town, village, street, church, store, or other places that may be closer to their lives and to their interests.

2. The first student begins with the name of a town. The second student needs to give the name of another town. The third student continues with the name of a new town. And it continues with the other members.

3. When one cannot give any name, he or she is out of the game. The activity continues until there is only one player remaining who knows more towns. And he or she will be the winner of that round of the game.

4. To make the game more sustainable, the teacher may need to work as a "moderator."

Intermediate Learners

1. Repeat Steps 1-4.

2. For intermediate learners, the themes in Step 2 may include state and regional information being introduced in social studies. The themes may also include places they have traveled to or learned from movies, TV, books, or other adults.

Advanced Learners

1. After the students form a game group, the teacher assigns a theme or students are allowed to decide on the theme. For example: countries in South and Central America.

2. To make the game more competitive, the members may change the second rule with the beginning learners as follows: The first student begins

with the name of any country. The second student needs to give the name of another country that begins with the last letter in the previous name. The third student continues with the name of a new country, which in turn begins with the last letter of the previous name. And it continues with the other members. This may require a larger theme, like countries in the Southern Hemisphere or rivers of the world.

3. The game may also be adapted for use with the whole class into a quiz-type activity. For example, the teacher may divide the class into two teams, and then ask them to study the relevant themes as a team. Instead of playing the game as individuals, the team members may work together and come up with answers against members in the other team. The team that remembers the most place names will be the winner.

Curriculum Connections

To make the game more closely related to the current focus of students' social studies or geography classes, the game may be adapted to focus on particular areas, e.g., U.S. national or state geography; European, Asian, or African geography. The teacher may also use flash cards or study the map of the area with students before the game, or review the cards/map after the game.

STRATEGY 17
Storytelling

This strategy provides opportunities for students to read multicultural stories or folklore and retell what they read. Specifically, each student will be able to choose a story to read from a culture he or she is interested in exploring. Then, the student will share his or her story with the other students in the class by retelling the story. Besides helping students to read multicultural literature, this strategy offers advanced students opportunities to present their ideas orally in front of an audience.

ELA Standard: 12

Beginning and Intermediate Learners

1. The teacher begins by explaining that each student will choose a multicultural book to read independently. (The teacher may need to guide the student to choose a book at his or her reading level so that the student may understand the content.) After the reading, each student will share the story he or she read with other students in a small group.

2. The teacher provides a list of multicultural books for the students to choose from. For example, *All Night, All Day: A Child's First Book of African American Spirituals* (Bryan, A.); *Tar Beach* (Ringgold, F.); *Ali, Child of the Desert* ((London, J.; Ill. Lewin, T.); *Cornrows* (Yarbrough, C.), *The Seven Chinese Brothers* (Mahy, M.); *The Magic Fan* (Baker, K.); *The Trip Back Home* (Wong, J.); *The Golden Flower* (Jaffe, N.); *Cendrillon: A Caribbean Cinderella* (San Souci, R.; Ill. Pinckney, B.); *The Most Beautiful Place in the World* (Cameron, A.; Ill. Allen, T.B.); *Dream Catcher* (Osofsky, A.); *Where the Buffaloes Begin* (Baker, O.; Ill. Gammell, S.); *Thunder Magic* (Strete, C. K.).

3. Each student finds his or her own multicultural book to read (the books chosen need to be approved by the teacher).

4. The students are divided into groups of four, and each student retells the story he or she read with the other members.

5. The students are encouraged to give a dramatic retelling and may use the actual book during the retelling. The students need to take some notes or make an outline to help organize their retelling. The teacher walks around and facilitates the retelling.

Advanced Learners

1. Repeat Steps 1–5.

2. Each student writes down an outline of the story he or she read.

3. The students may use a simple handout, a dramatic read-aloud of a section, PowerPoint, visual objects, or any other form that helps to convey the ideas of the story.

4. After all the retelling is completed, the students put together a list of multicultural books to be read (and retold).

Curriculum Connections

This strategy may be used in ELA class across grade levels. Reading and retelling multicultural stories help students to develop their reading, as well as a keener sense of literary and cultural diversity. The teacher may also ask students to write down what they read and retold to make the reading, speaking, and writing connections. In addition to being useful for literacy learning, this strategy may help all students appreciate the colorful and rich literary traditions and cultural experiences around the world.

3

Multicultural Literature Events: Motivating Literacy Learning in Content Areas

STRATEGY 18
Literature: Celebrate Famous People From Diverse Backgrounds

Historical fiction, biographies of famous people, and biographies of people who contributed research to particular content areas all help students understand that content areas originated through the work of real people. This kind of study brings realism and authenticity to a subject area. Students can analyze individual perceptions of the world through the eyes of famous people and see how those perceptions shaped their contributions in their respective fields. Critically analyzing productive individuals' lives and accomplishments helps students see their own strengths and needs and recognize the characteristics of present and future leaders (Hopkinson, 2001; Kurtz, 2001). These famous people are models for our students. The following are a few examples:

- *Mary Anning and the Sea Dragon* (1999) is the story of her discovery of the fossil, ichthyosaurus.
- *Starry Messenger* (1996) relates Galileo's triumphs and tragedies.

- *Wilma Unlimited* (1994) is an African American Olympic runner's story.
- *My Dream of Martin Luther King* (1995) is a brief story of the great American hero and leader of the Civil Rights Movement.
- *Diego Rivera* (1989) is a depiction of the great Mexican muralist and political activist.
- *Sacajawea* (1987) presents the story of the Native American woman who guided Lewis and Clark on their expedition in western North America.
- *Girl Wonder, A Baseball Story in Nine Innings* (2003) is the triumphant true account of a female athlete.

ELA Standard: 3

Beginning Learners

1. Students retell the story of the person.

2. Students create a class storybook about favorite people. Each student draws a picture and writes a sentence or two about the famous person. Then laminate it.

3. Make the storybook a part of the class library and practice reading it in pairs.

4. Students take it home to read to family members.

Intermediate Learners

1. Reads the book to the class and uses reader response activities explained in Strategy 21.

2. Students create the clothing of the famous people in the dress-up center or by drawing/coloring the clothing.

3. Students reenact the life story as the teacher reads the picture book.

4. Create a readers' theater production and videotape it for other classes to view.

5. Encourage students to talk about how they are similar to the people studied in physical appearance, life stories, interests, and dreams.

Advanced Learners

1. Students read books in literature circles and tell life stories by presenting major events in the biographies.

2. Students as a group create a biographical lifeline of a particular person.

3. Students research other sources to find more information.

4. Students create a work of art or three-dimensional object representing the person.

5. Students individually write a paragraph explaining why this person is famous and a positive contributor to our world.

Curriculum Connections

This strategy works for any content area. The teacher is required to find the famous people in a particular content area. These activities are especially influential on days before and after vacations or as a break from typical classroom practice. These activities motivate students, and they begin to see the relationship between a content area and real-life experiences.

Teachers' Comments

"Students love to take the books home. They are always in demand."

"What better way than teach the students about role models from their diverse community/background."

"All of my students were eager to be involved. This strategy reaches everyone in the class."

STRATEGY 19
Literature in Mathematics

A piece of youth literature in a mathematics class brings depth to understanding and an appreciation for the fact that mathematics is a worldwide endeavor that has been a part of all civilizations. There are many multicultural mathematics books written with great historical interest and humor. Teachers may read these books as a way to draw upon prior knowledge, but also to develop an interest in mathematics. Many of the picture books have high-level concepts in them, thus helping to diminish anxiety in older students.

ELA Standard: 3

Beginning Learners

1. When studying a particular unit in mathematics, creating a center with appropriate literature shows students that mathematics and literacy development go hand in hand.

2. For example, using *The Village of Round and Square Houses* and *City by the Numbers*, encourages students to look at their surroundings to find geometric shapes and repeating patterns.

3. Reading these books, followed by discussions, will raise questions that can be recorded and then answered with school building or local field trips.

4. Additionally, a disposable camera sent home to photograph shapes in and around the children's homes can add to understanding mathematics everywhere.

5. Discussion of different cultures such as city, farm, and structures in other countries increases awareness of mathematics as being everywhere.

The following are some possible examples of books:

Anno, M., *Anno's Journey*

Anno, M., *Anno's Mysterious Multiplying Jar*

Anno, M., *Anno's Spain*

Burns, M., *Spaghetti and Meatballs for All!*

Grifalconi, A., *The Village of Round and Square Houses*

Johnson, S. T., *City by Numbers*

Murphy, S. J., *Betcha!*

Murphy, S. J., *Divide and Ride*

Murphy, S. J. *Give Me Half!*

Myller, R., *How Big Is a Foot?*

Tompert, A. *Grandfather Tang's Story*

Intermediate to Advanced Learners

1. Reading stories about famous mathematicians and cultures that have been mathematically oriented are ways to spark interest, encourage punctuality, and develop an understanding of mathematical concepts. The Internet provides wonderful leads on famous mathematicians from different cultures.

2. Students may want to borrow illustrated youth literature to read to younger siblings.

3. An illustrated multicultural mathematics book may be assigned as a first step before searching for more information on the Web. All can be shared with the class.

4. A classroom area to display the picture books gives students opportunities to browse.

5. Many of the picture books explain mathematical concepts in ways that help students understand.

6. Students may create and design their own mathematics books to be shared in other classrooms and with younger audiences.

The following are examples of books to stimulate the above activities that use mathematics picture books as a strategy for motivating interest in mathematics and giving a greater depth of understanding of mathematical concepts.

Burns, M., *The Greedy Triangle*

Heller, R., *More Geometrics*

Neuschwander, C., *Sir Cumference and the First Round Table*

Scieszka, J., *Math Curse*

Schwartz, D., *How Much Is a Million?*

Tang, Greg, *Math-terpieces*

Tang, G., *The Grapes of Math*

Tang, Greg, *Math for All Seasons*

Wisniewski, D., *Rain Player*

Curriculum Connections

These pieces of literature can be tied to cultures around the world. They enhance the study of mathematics with humor and delightful stories and illustrations. They bring added joy to the study of mathematics while encouraging related reading, writing, listening, speaking, and viewing.

Teachers' Comments

"I never thought to use picture books in my math classes. It motivates kids."

"Math comes alive using picture books. Students like to make their own math books as well."

"My ELL students thrive when I use picture books."

STRATEGY 20
Appreciation of the Arts

An understanding and appreciation of cultures is often taught through the arts. Working with the school's art, music, and drama teachers may help enrich this strategy. Also, local musicians and artists can be additional resources. Seeing and listening to artistic endeavors may inspire the students to think about their own talents.

ELA Standard: 2

Beginning Learners

1. Picture books are a means of introducing students to various art media. Encourage the students to choose what they like and try to make it in their own way, e.g., I like that tree in the picture. I am going to make one that is sort of like that tree. I like the colors in that picture. I am going to use those colors in my picture. I like that statue of a dolphin. I am going to make a little one with this clay.

2. Musicians or older students may visit the class to talk about various musical instruments and play short pieces of music with instruments from different cultures—steel drums, sitar, maracas, flute. Students may want to touch and play these instruments.

3. Local theater groups may be invited to perform and actually teach students about mime and other forms of acting.

4. A costume corner or center may be a place where the actors decide what is authentic for a particular theater or dance production.

5. Local dancers from Latino, Arabic, African, or Asian cultures may perform in classrooms and teach the students dance steps using music from the cultures.

6. Students may present a performance entitled *Appreciating the Arts Around the World* for the local community.

Intermediate and Advanced Learners

All of the above activities are appropriate along with the following:

1. Read *Honoring Our Ancestors: Stories and Pictures by Fourteen Artists* (1999) and *Just Like Me: Self-Portraits of Fourteen Artists* (1997). Each student may select an artist to study in *Just Like Me,* and be ready to tell the life story. Also, students can try to recreate a sample of their work.

2. Read *Cricket in Times Square* (1988). The Bellini family's favorite opera is *Aida.* Listen to parts of the opera and view parts of the video. Then read the 1997 picture book called *Aida,* illustrated by Diane and Leo Dillon. Leontyne Price tells her story and the story of Aida. (The illustrations

are fabulous.) This entire experience will allow students to learn something of New York City, Italian opera, ancient Egyptian culture, and a famous African American diva.

3. Study Diego Rivera murals and any other local murals using the KWLQ format described in Strategy 44. Then, with the help of the art teacher and other interested community members, create a class or school mural depicting significant recent historical events in the community, nation, and world. This could be long-term and permanent with the necessary commitment from educational and community leaders. It could also be a class project that graces the hallways for a few months.

Curriculum Connections

The curriculum connections are many and varied. Reading, writing, listening, speaking, and viewing are significant to all activities in this strategy. Also, mathematics will come into play with perspectives on other pieces of art and the potential mural. Music, of course, is naturally mathematical regarding rhythm and timing. Social studies relates to theater in that the plays may likely relate to diverse groups of the world's peoples as well as historical events. Additionally, social studies relates to the artist and what he or she creates at a particular time in history. History often influences art. Sound and color mixes can be analyzed scientifically. Historically, the arts are reflections of all aspects of communities and nations.

Teachers' Comments

"I could never think of a good reason to connect with the art and music teachers. This strategy showed me how."

"The best in my kids comes out when I bring in the art and music. I'll do this again and again in the years to come."

"The music and art generated excitement not usually seen in my classroom."

STRATEGY 21
Literature in History

Students learn about the history of their communities, our nation, and other nations through picture books. This helps them develop an appreciation for their own community and the communities of others in our nation and world. Picture books use the visual to teach not only information, but the aesthetic value of various art media.

ELA Standard: 2

Beginning and Intermediate Learners

1. Read about urban, rural, and suburban communities in picture books such as:
   Barbour, K., *Little Nino's Pizzeria*
   Barracca, D., & S., *The Adventures of Taxi Dog*
   Garrett, A., *Keeper of the Swamp*
   Jakobsen, K., *My New York*
   Loomis, C., *Across America, I Love You,*
   MacDonald, S., *Sea Shapes*
   Myers, W. D., *Harlem*
   Pack, L., *A is for Appalachia*
   Shelton, C., *San Antonio: The Wayward River*
   Swope, S., *The Araboolies of Liberty Street*

2. Teachers give students disposable cameras to take pictures of the outsides of their homes and other important places in their community.

3. Teachers bring in picture books that deal with the history of their region and talk about how the area has changed and why it has changed.
   Anderson, W., *Pioneer Girl: The Story of Laura Ingalls Wilder*
   Bruchac, J., *Native American Stories*
   Cherry, L., *A River Ran Wild*
   Cherry, L., *The Armadillo From Amarillo*
   Hopkinson, D., *Sweet Clara and the Freedom Quilt*
   Osofsky, A., *Dreamcatcher*

4. Community visitors, such as members of the local historical society, local librarian, and grandparents and great-grandparents tell about the past history of the community.

5. Students create before and after pictures of the community individually, in pairs, or in a class mural.

Intermediate and Advanced Learners

1. All of the above may be modified for intermediate as a starting point.

2. Then, students may study the following picture books concerning other nations in the world and their histories, drawing from the continents of Asia, Africa, Europe, and South America.

3. The following books are examples:
   Angelou, M., *Kofi and His Magic*
   Chang, M., *Story of the Chinese Zodiac*
   Chao, L., *Stories From Mencius*
   Cherry, L., & Plotkin, M., *The Shaman's Apprentice*
   Grutman, J. H., *The Ledgerbook of Thomas Blue Eagle*
   Kita, S., *Three Whales: Who Won the Heart of the World*
   Kunin, C., *My Hanukkah Alphabet*
   London, J., *Ali, Student of the Desert*
   Mayer, M., *Baba Yaga and Vasilisa the Brave*
   Musgrove, M., *Ashanti to Zulu: African Traditions*
   Sabuda, R., *Tutankamen's Gift*
   Schimmel, S., *Students of the Earth . . . Remember*
   Sis, P., *Tibet: Through the Red Box*
   Tan, A., *The Moon Lady*
   Unobagha, U., *Off to the Sweet Shores of Africa*
   Wisniewski, D., *Rain Player*

4. Students can see how our nation may have developed due to the contributions of the nations and people of other parts of the world.

5. The following books are examples:
   Hearne, B., *Seven Brave Women*
   Jassem, K., *Sacajawea: Wilderness Guide*
   Krull, K., *Wilma Unlimited*
   Martin, J. B., *Snowflake Bentley*
   Petit, J., *Maya Angelou: Journey of the Heart*
   Price, L., *Aida*
   Provensen, A., *My Fellow Americans*
   Rohmer, H., *Honoring Our Ancestors*
   Tompert, A., *Grandfather Tang's Story*

   Next, immigration study naturally will occur. The following books are examples:
   Bunting, E., *How Many Days to America?*
   Hoose, P., *We Were There, Too!*
   Hopkinson, D., *Shutting Out the Sky*
   Moss, M., *Hannah's Journal*
   Polacco, P., *The Keeping Quilt*
   Rohmer, H., *Honoring Our Ancestors*
   Say, A., *Grandfather's Journey*
   Rosenblum, R., *Journey to the Golden Land*

6. Students can see how our nation developed due to the contributions of diverse groups of people who inhabited the continent, and people from nations around the world who came to North America.

7. Native Americans visit the classroom to tell about their contributions to the development of the United States. They will also be explaining their perspectives on American history. Before they arrive, be sure to read

texts related to the Native American group. The school librarian and local historical society can help. Students will prepare questions for the visitors.

Grutman, J. H., *The Ledgerbook of Thomas Blue Eagle*
McGovern, A., . . . *If You lived With the Sioux Indians*
Quiri, P. R., *The Algonquians*
Renner, M., *The Girl Who Swam With the Fish*
Rhoads, D., *The Corn Grows Ripe*
Rodanas, K., *Dragonfly's Tale*
Wood, N., *Dancing Moons*

8. Visitors from other nations come into the classroom to tell about their own experiences of coming to the United States. Students read about the nations they emigrated from and have prepared questions for the visitors. The answers are recorded.

9. Students visit a local art museum, historical society museum, and local historical site. Write and illustrate it.

10. Students create an illustrated local or national history that includes the contributions of the diverse groups of people. The book is bound and placed in the school library.

Curriculum Connections

Studying history through literature helps students see the struggles and triumphs of diverse groups of people as they create and develop communities. It demonstrates, in an aesthetic manner, what should be memorable. If we are to learn from history, the understanding and appreciation of diverse perspectives and cultures are essential.

Teachers' Comments

"The literature motivates students; they remember what they are studying."
"ELL students are given the visuals they need."
"Our kids love pictures no matter the grade level."

STRATEGY 22
Literature in Science

Science and mathematics are all around us. To help students understand how meaningful these content areas are, it is important to help them see the relevance in their own lives as well as the community's life. Students may connect in many ways with the help of family and community. Teachers can invite community or family members to various content area classes. Students might consider future occupations more seriously when they hear from community or family members. A pride in family and community work emerges in the process, and also gives relevance to the content areas.

ELA Standards: 1 and 4

1. Read through student registration cards to determine what kinds of work family members do. Mechanics and repair people know about simple machines. Nurse's aides and doctors know about the human body systems. Carpenters and architects understand many principles of trigonometry related to framing and designing homes. Cooks and pharmacists know a lot about chemical change. Electricians and engineers have knowledge about what powers our world. (Companies will often allow workers to go to a school as part of their public relations programs.)

2. At the beginning of a unit of study, ask students who they know in these occupations. In class, list the people and discuss the occupations. Encourage students to invite family members to discuss their work. If this doesn't work, make phone calls and send letters to invite family and community members to class.

3. At the end of a unit of study, discuss other occupations that might relate to the content of mathematics and science.

Beginners to Intermediate Learners

The following are specific examples of people who may visit the class. Of course, there are many more.

TAKE-APART DAYS—SIMPLE MACHINES AND PHYSICS

1. Ask students to bring in mechanical devices that no longer work, such as old toasters, irons, radios, and electric coffeepots.

2. Invite family members who work with tools to come into school to help students take apart these old machines to discover what is inside.

3. Have students draw the object and label each part. As they discover what is inside, students draw and label what they think it is.

4. Students report discoveries to the class.

5. Some groups may want to try to fix the appliances.

6. Find the simple machines that make complex motors.

RESPIRATORY SYSTEM—BIOLOGY

1. Invite a family member or members who have stopped smoking.

2. Persons talk about the stopping process.

3. Students interview them about their feelings, physical and emotional.
   Interview Questions:
   When did you start?
   Where did you start?
   Why did you start?
   How long did you smoke?
   How do you feel?

4. After the people leave, students discuss the interviews and write/draw about the lungs of the people interviewed.

Intermediate to Advanced Learners

The following are specific examples of people who may visit the class. Of course, there are many more.

INVITE A PROFESSIONAL COOK TO CHEMISTRY CLASS

1. The cook discusses the various ingredients used in cooking, such as baking soda, sugar, vinegar, yeast, salt, and more. The cook tells what these chemicals do.

2. Students record how these ingredients are used to prepare food.

3. Demonstrate chemical reactions in food preparation, for example, carbon, sodium chloride, acetic acid, and sodium hydroxide. Discuss chemical formulas.

4. Write the formulas for the various chemicals used in cooking.

INVITE A CARPENTER TO MATHEMATICS CLASS

1. Students study plans for a home in relation to trigonometry.

2. The carpenter shows and explains tools used to build homes.

3. The carpenter actually builds a small frame in the classroom from 2×4 wood.

4. Students prepare questions ahead to be given to the carpenter to discuss with the class.

5. Students study more complex house plans and what is necessary to pursue carpentry.

6. Students build a balsa wood or straw structure using angles.

Curriculum Connections

Reading, writing, listening, speaking, and viewing are all parts of these culturally responsive mathematics and science strategies. Students will link their community to the units of study and see the relevance of the lessons to their own lives. They will meet people from differing backgrounds and experiences who make significant contributions to the community. The people invited could contribute to almost any age group. Be sure to let them know before they arrive in class what you and the students expect from the visit.

Teachers' Comments

"This takes time to plan, but it is so successful. The following year it was much easier, because I knew where to go and who to ask."

"I never thought this would work this well. I wouldn't have done this if it wasn't an assignment for a grad class. I'll keep doing this."

"The pride that the kids and the parents showed was worth a million bucks."

STRATEGY 23
Exploration of Values: Reader Response to Diversity

Exploration of values through literature is based on the reader-response perspective (Rosenblatt, 1982). This theory proposes that the reader is essential to the interpretation of literary experiences. Additionally, personal reactions to literature help the reader relate to and bring meaning to the story. Student readers from diverse backgrounds and experiences are stimulated to respond through personal expression and activities. This gives relevance to teaching and learning in classrooms.

When students respond to literature, they explain their unique responses and support those responses in cognitive and affective ways. The readers may not only write about and talk about a response, they may also use music and other art forms to express their unique responses (Hynds, 1997).

ELA Standard: 2

Beginning Learners

1. Begin with visual images from students' literature, such as *Play Gently, Alfie Bear* by Walters (2001)—an early childhood story with pictures depicting mama bear teaching little bear cubs to be gentle with baby bear. Relate this story to gentle play and actions at home and at school.

2. *Mufaro's Beautiful Daughters: An African Tale* by Steptoe (1987) concerns the rewards for being kind. This Cinderella story regards true beauty as the willingness to care for others. It can be compared and contrasted with other similar folk tales from around the world, such as *The Egyptian Cinderella* (1989), *The Korean Cinderella* (1993), *The Irish Cinderlad* (1996), *The Persian Cinderella* (1999), and *Angkat: The Cambodian Cinderella* (1998). Using Cinderella stories from around the world exposes young people to similarities and differences that encourage reader responses that are similar and different.

3. Reader response lends itself to the following activities:
   – Students talk about the faces and feelings.
   – Look at the sizes of individuals portrayed in the pictures and discuss importance.
   – Look at dress, setting, and reaction.
   – Who is happy? Who is sad?
   – Where are they?
   – What are they doing?
   – How are they talking?

4. Class murals pull similarities and differences together—begin portions of the murals at various group sites after class discussions. (Art teacher may want to help with this project.)

5. Acting out the stories is a joyous response using classroom props from a costume or dress-up corner gathered at the beginning of the school year from families and community members. (Always check for cleanliness.)

Intermediate and Advanced Learners

1. All of the above are appropriate for advanced learners, but additional steps might be to study Web sites, and photojournalism. Trade books, such as young adult novels related to language arts and other content areas, are ideal for reader-response activities that help students develop their aesthetic (reading for pleasure) and efferent (reading for information) reading/thinking. Examples with particular content areas are

   Creech, S. *Walk Two Moons*—Social Studies, English, Science, Mathematics
   Curtis, C. P. *The Watsons Go to Birminghaam*—Social Studies, English, Math, Music
   Flake, S. *The Skin I'm In*—Social Studies, English
   Fox, P. *Monkey Island*—Social Studies, English, Science
   Konisburg, E. I. *A View From Saturday*—Social Studies
   Kurtz, J. *The Storytellers Beads*—Social Studies, English
   Lowry, L. *The Giver*—Science, Social Studies, Math
   O'Dell, S. *Island of the Blue Dolphin*—Social Studies, Math, Science
   Speare, E. G., *Witch of Blackbird Pond*—Social Studies, Math, Science, English
   Yep, L. *Dragonwings*—Social Studies, Math, Science, English, Art
   Yolen, J. *Devil's Arithmetic*—Math, Social Studies, Science, English

2. Discussions should take place in small groups to study the following:

   Authors' background to discover perspective—What are major events in the author's life story? Where did and does the author reside? Who were and are the author's people influences?

   Analyze purpose—Why did the author write/record the story? Who is the author's audience?

   Analyze similarities and differences between and among the people.

3. Create a song, poem, story, or art form about an individual or book.

Curriculum Connections

Reader response develops critical thinking in all content areas. It personalizes learning, validates prior knowledge, and motivates students in a risk-free learning community. Language arts, social studies, and art classes lend themselves to this strategy.

Teachers' Comments

"For ELL students, I substituted picture books with similar themes as the trade books. They were placed in specific group discussions and showed their material. Their classmates asked questions about the pictures and talked about their books in relation to the picture book."

"Students get into the books when given different ways to respond to the literature."

"Student individual responses are valued and that's a classroom value in and of itself."

STRATEGY 24
Math Expression and Everyday Language

This strategy links students' literacy learning with math. By helping students understand that math problems may be related to "real" situations and math expressions may be captured in everyday language, students are helped to think that math is itself a special form of language that has its own logic and way of reasoning. By making the lessons more fun and engaging, the teacher may generate more interest for students to study math.

ELA Standard: 12

Beginning and Intermediate Learners

1. The teacher may begin with the classic Chinese story of how Cao Chong weighed the elephant: In ancient China, there was an emperor called Cao Cao. One day, his Indian friend sent him a huge elephant as a gift. Curious about how heavy the elephant would be, the emperor could not find a way to weigh the elephant because there was no modern scale at that time. The teacher pauses here and directs the following question to the students: How may the elephant be weighed?

2. The teacher continues with the following. The emperor's young son, Cao Chong, thought of an idea. First, he had people lead the elephant onto a boat and mark down the watermark on the side of the boat. Then, after the elephant was taken off the boat, he had big rocks taken onto the boat, until the watermark reached the same level as when the elephant was on the boat. By weighing the rocks separately and adding up the total weight, he figured out how heavy the elephant was.

3. Mathematically stated, the results may be put as: The weight of rock 1 + rock 2 + rock 3 . . . + rock n = the weight of the elephant.

Advanced Learners

1. Repeat Steps 1–3.

2. After the above brain teaser, the teacher tells the classic Arab math problem to be solved by the students. "A dairy farmer died and left all his 17 cows to his three sons. In his will, he gave one-half of his cows to his eldest child, one-third of his cows to his second child, and one-ninth of his cows to his youngest child. As 17 cannot be divided by two, three, or nine, the three children did not know how to divide the cows among them. Can you figure out a way to help them out?"

3. After giving some time for the students to think about how to divide the cows, the teacher may pretend to be the children's generous uncle who suggested adding one of his own cows to make it 18. Thus, one-half of 18 is 9, one-third of 18 is 6, one-ninth of 18 is 2. That is exactly the

number of cows each child inherited, and the uncle's one cow was still his to keep.

4. Next, the teacher asks the students to add up $1/2 + 1/3 + 1/9$ to see whether they come to be 1, or 100 percent of the total number of cows. After the students get it as 17/18, the teacher points out that the children's dead father (or their wise uncle) had already figured this out.

5. The teacher helps the students to come up with the math equation for this puzzle: $1/2 + 1/3 + 1/9 \neq 1$. (As students in Grades 6 through 8 have already learned fractions, they should be able to work out the reasoning behind the division, instead of relying on the teacher's explanation.)

6. The puzzle may be expressed graphically, as shown below.

Curriculum Connections

This strategy may be used in ELA and math classes. Many students find math uninteresting and difficult, and the results of standardized tests in math are unsatisfactory. It is imperative for teachers to make their lessons creative and engaging. If students may be helped to understand that mathematical reasoning is a way of meaning-making, as is language, they perhaps can become less intimidated by math problems and more willing to put in the effort for learning. When students learn to think across the curriculum, they will grow linguistically and mathematically.

Division of the Cows

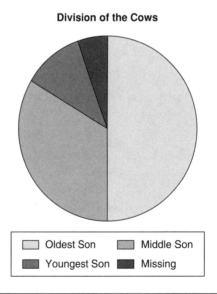

| Oldest Son | Middle Son |
| Youngest Son | Missing |

4

Critical
Media Literacy:
Exploring Values

STRATEGY 25
Introduction to Critical Media Literacy

Daily, students spend 5.5 hours, on average, engaged in media forms outside of school (PBS Adult Learning Service, 1999). The implicit and explicit messages conveyed by the media formulate population opinions and ideas. In particular, large-scale media impact studies link media exposure to social outcomes, such as violence, obesity, substance abuse, and materialism, to name a few. Therefore it is essential for educators in a democratic society to assist youth in the development of critical thinking in regard to media that bombard them daily with images and words that influence their thinking and acting (Schmidt & Pailliotet, 2001). This strategy will encourage students to study the media and begin to question its value in terms of the diverse ideas expressed in classroom discussions.

Teachers who use culturally responsive teaching strategies can easily help their students think critically about texts and other print materials. Student perspectives and cultures have an impact on how they view print and pictures, so analyzing these media forms brings their lives into understanding and acquiring the content (Laier, Edwards, McMillon, & Turner, 2001).

ELA Standards: 4 and 8

1. Picture books, newspapers, Web sites, textbooks, and magazines can be analyzed using the following brief outline.

DESCRIBE, QUESTION, and EVALUATE

1. Describe what you see—everything, such as print shape and size, position, action, dialogue, culture, and processes.

2. Ask questions, interpret, and respond to what you see.

3. Evaluate and apply what you see. Purpose is questioned and inferences made.

Activities could begin with materials from home, such as a favorite advertisement or picture book.

Beginning and Intermediate Learners

1. *Advertisements.* Ask students to discuss their favorite advertisements. Have them bring in their favorite snack containers, toys, clothing, and video ads from home.

2. They can talk about why they buy the items.

3. Teachers create lessons around the amount of money spent.

4. Teachers create graphing lessons around time spent listening to and viewing media advertisements.

5. Students create ads that talk back to the ads they've seen or heard.

6. The class tracks media images of diverse groups of people, such as the Arabic peoples. How are they represented? Are the images stereotypical?

7. Students study supermarkets and toy stores to discover where items are placed. They record the kinds of items being sold to young people. Consider where certain items are located and why.

Intermediate and Advanced Learners

1. *Newspapers.* Analyzing the news throughout the year is a daily means for practicing critical media literacy.

2. Compare and contrast newspaper articles and newscasts.

3. Follow a news story from beginning to end.

4. Keep a world map showing where major news stories are occurring to get an idea how much world, local, and national news is covered daily.

5. Talk about varying perspectives or ways of seeing and interpreting the world.

6. The picture books below relate to particular content areas.
   Bunting, E., *How Many Days to America*—Social Studies, 21st Century
   Burns, M., *The Greedy Triangle*—Mathematics
   Cherry, L., *The River Ran Wild*—Science and Environmental

Maruki, T., *Hiroshima Non Pika*—Social Studies, 20th Century

Miller, W., *Tituba*—Language Arts, Bridge to *The Crucible*

7. *Software.* Have students analyze software used in the classroom by looking at gender, voice, culture, violence, the blurring of fantasy and reality, winning is everything, fast is good, and slow is punishable.

8. *Web sites.* Analyzing Web sites can be revealing. Students may get a variety of perspectives at a particular site. For instance, when typing in the subject "Iraqi women," numerous testimonies appear telling of their power, based on the Code of Hammurabi, and also, stories appear relating to the poor treatment of women written by those whose husbands had been exiled by Saddam Hussein.

9. *Magazines.* These forms of media are particularly compelling. Their beautiful glossy pictures capture attention, with the fuzzy lens making people appear physically perfect. Study what they are selling.

Curriculum Connections

Once a teacher begins to help students engage in critical media literacy, the students begin to see the numerous perspectives that surround them. They also begin to decide what is important and what isn't important. All the above activities will encourage youth to think in greater depth, to question more freely, and to see more clearly. It is important to remember that home, school, and community connections cannot be ignored when developing critical media literacy.

Teachers' Comments

"We have an obligation to our students to help them become critical consumers of the media. This strategy helps us do that."

"Students are so interested, because they spend so much time with the media."

"We might as well make use of it. It's not going away."

STRATEGY 26
Critical Media Literacy and Literature: Understanding Family, School, and Community Values

Knowing family and community values is key to connecting literature with critical media literacy (Laier, Edwards, McMillon, & Turner, 2001). As teachers are forming relationships with students in their classrooms, they should be simultaneously reaching out to the families and communities of their students. Creating intimate connections with families helps to develop culturally sensitive pedagogy (Ladson-Billings, 1995). Also, dealing effectively with classroom diversity encourages the appreciation of differences that helps students see other perspectives.

Sharing family and community stories, encouraging family and community member visits, studying family and community artifacts, celebrating family and community photos, and analyzing multicultural literature are all ways to develop real relationships among home, community, and school members (Edwards, Pleasants, & Franklin, 1999; Leftwich, 2002). The newsletter is fine as an ancillary product, but should not serve as the main vehicle for making connections. Authentic communication and the sharing of values begin with person-to-person contact (Schmidt, 2001).

ELA Standard: 4 and 9

Beginning/Intermediate/Advanced Learners

1. No matter what the age or stage, illustrated books are motivating. If the message is powerful, students of all ability levels, K–8, are motivated to listen and comment.

2. Share the values in multicultural literature by asking questions about pictures, the ways people are behaving or acting. There are hundreds of examples, and the following are a few favorites:

    Chrysanthemum (1991) is about a student who has difficulties with her name in school.

    Whoever You Are (1997) shows and celebrates students with different languages, cultures, abilities, and skin colors.

    The Story of Ruby Bridges (1995) is the recounting of the life of the student who changed school segregation.

    Grandfather's Journey (1994) is a poignant story of an immigrant's cultural conflict.

    People (1980) is a humorous and interesting picture book of the world's people. It includes languages, homes, food, play, dress, and religion, with an emphasis on the wonder of human differences.

    The Araboolies of Liberty Street (1989) is a humorous story of unusual people who move into a pristine neighborhood where all the homes and people appear to be alike.

    Sadako (1993) is the story of a boy who lives in Hiroshima and who gets the radiation-related cancer from the atomic bomb.

    Dreamcatcher (1992) gives the reader a view of life concerning the heritage of Native Americans.

3. Other activities may include:
   - Create concept maps about books that exhibit family values such as courage, sharing, helping, and caring.
   - Role-play values and dramatize them in performances around the literature.
   - Compare and contrast people in the literature with people in the classroom and news, using Venn diagrams.
   - Share and compare and contrast media literacy materials from home and school, such as magazines, newspapers, books, calendars, photos, etc. Discuss how they are used. (An African American home may have hymnals and prayers practiced, memorized, and sung.)
   - Retell a story told by Grandma or someone in the family and compare and contrast it with a story read in school.
   - Invite community and family members to talk about their work and the literacy materials they use at work.

Curriculum Connections

These literature/language arts and critical media links not only assist in the development of critical media literacy, but also strengthen the home, school, and community connections for literacy development.

Teachers' Comments

"Once students realize that picture books are not 'baby books,' they get involved."

"This is a way to talk about the richness of differences. I always use picture books in my eighth-grade classes. All learners benefit from the aesthetic value of the books."

"Reading levels are often not a problem with picture books. Everyone gets into them."

STRATEGY 27
Deep Viewing and the Visual Media

Today our young people engage with mass media by watching films, CDs, videos, and television. Also, they surf the Web and play electronic games, as well as interact with billboards, books, comics, and other visual media. We know that by age six, our students have seen hundreds of thousands of visual advertisements. We know that by the time a student graduates from high school, he or she has spent more time watching television than in classrooms (Schmidt & Pailliotet, 2001). Many of the images students receive help them develop definite ideas about our culture and the people in it. This can be both good and bad in that some ads may encourage us to go on to higher education, while others may encourage overeating. Some television programs or films may give us a better understanding of a news event, while others may help to develop stereotypes about certain groups of people in our nation and world.

Deep Viewing was developed by Ann Watts Pailliotet (1999) to help us become critical viewers of the visual media. She created a sequence of coding categories to help our young people analyze visual media and think about their own ideas as well as the ideas of others. This strategy can be modified for beginning and intermediate learners. It will certainly help students think about what they are seeing and how it may influence their thinking.

Coding Categories for Advanced Deep Viewing

Category	What Is Included	Questions to Ask
Action/Sequence (time relationship)	Order, content, and duration of events	What happens? What order? When and for how long?
Designs/Forms (visual meaning units)	Characteristics of objects, icons, graphics, visual content	Who/what is pictured? What are the characteristics of people and objects?
Actors/Discourse (words and phrases)	How written and spoken language convey content; actual message, tone, pitch, rate	What is said and by whom? How is it said and heard?
Proximity/Movement (directionality)	Use of space and all movements, including gestures, relative size	How is space used? What types of movements occur?

Coding Categories for Advanced Deep Viewing

Category	What Is Included	Questions to Ask
Culture/Context (references to cultural knowledge)	Point of view, assumptions related to understanding based on "common" knowledge stereotypes	To whom might this video be targeted? What symbols do you notice? What is implied? What is missing?
Effects/Processes (production devices, visual and audio)	How production elements and quality affect meaning	What is seen? What is missing? What is the quality

Follow the above coding and complete Deep Viewing on the following:

1. Select favorite television programs.

2. Select Web sites.

3. Select computer programs.

4. Electronic games.

5. Videos and/or CDs.

6. Films.

ELA Standards: 4 and 8

Beginning and Intermediate Learners

1. View the film *Finding Nemo* or an other popular culture video.

2. After the viewing, students and teacher record the order of major events.

3. Describe/draw main characters and talk about their ways of looking and behaving.

4. Explain the way they talk—act out parts and scenes as impromptu activities.

5. Discuss who likes this story and why.

6. Discuss most and least favorite parts and why.

7. What is the story teaching us? How can the story help us every day?

8. The message of Nemo might be, "Our families and communities care about their students and will travel far and wide to care for us." So a center

can be created for the students to write another story about themselves around this theme. The class may actually perform the story with costumes and scenery. It can then be videotaped and shown to other classes. Deep Viewing may be used to analyze the video.

Intermediate and Advanced Learners

1. The television provides a flashy fast pace, set to music. Its catchy slogans grab us as we view super toys, delicious food, fabulous cars, romantic interludes, humorous situations, and party scenes, all contributing to a "what life oughta be" attitude.

2. Discuss the development of differing communities and describe their characteristics and how the media affects them. In an elementary school, it might be easy to see how the media impacts a kindergartener and first grader and compare and contrast these effects with a fifth grader or a secondary school student.

3. Look at substance abuse and poor eating habits and how television advertisements affect the thinking of students and young people.

4. Analyze favorite television shows. What images do they present and how accurate are they? Do people really behave in those ways?

5. Ask students how the shows make them feel.

6. Have students how take photos of who they are and create bulletin boards, scrapbooks, and Web sites describing who they are.

7. In a whole group or small group, critically watch a cartoon, movie, or television program about violence and talk about its effects. (Be careful what you select. Be sure that parents know why you are showing what you are showing to your class.) Present the reading of excellent literature as an alternative to the television show.

Curriculum Connections

The old adage, "Seeing is believing," has caused great harm in learning the truth. In this age of bombardment by the visual media, people can become complacent and easily believe the chosen images presented to us. Therefore, Deep Viewing is a systematic means of analyzing all visual media and learning to question visual information in ways that will help us become critical thinkers. Deep Viewing is useful in all content areas because it can promote the kinds of questioning and thinking that help students actually learn new ways of understanding and open up new perspectives in content areas.

Teachers' Comments

"At first, I thought I wouldn't have time to do this, but I have to make time. It's too important. Our kids have to think about what they are seeing."

"This strategy covers all ELA standards."

"My kids get into it and keep talking about it."

STRATEGY 28
Textual and Visual Connections

This strategy provides students with opportunities to connect the written language with a personally meaningful visual image or physical object. The visual item may be a photograph, a drawing, a design, etc. The written response may take the form of a poem, a creative one-paragraph essay, or any other imaginative form. This strategy requires viewing and interpreting things from a personally meaningful perspective. Thinking about a physical object also helps to nurture an awareness of language as a mental tool for expressing meaning.

ELA Standard: 12

Beginning Learners

1. Each student will collect or create an object that is personally meaningful to the individual. For beginning learners, the object may include a toy, a photograph of a pet, a favorite book or dress, etc.

2. Instead of having beginning students compose a poem or write an essay, the teacher may just ask them to narrate, with the object in hand, what the object brings to mind.

Intermediate Learners

1. Intermediate learners who have more developed writing abilities may write short descriptive accounts about their objects.

2. Additionally, the teacher may use Steps 4 and 5 from the steps for advanced learners.

Advanced Learners

1. For advanced learners, the object collected may be a place visited, some gear for a sport, a personal diary, a favorite book, or a photograph of one's best friend.

2. Each student thinks about some interesting ways to capture the unique qualities or characteristics of his or her own object and write them down in a short poem, one-paragraph essay, or creative lyrics. English Language Learners may be given the option of using symbolic expressions, metaphors, or creative language.

3. To help the students get started, the teacher may model the steps of the activity by showing a personal object and reciting its related written representation. For example, a teacher may bring in a photo of Niagara Falls, which was captured by the short poem below.

4. After all students finish their writing, the written representation, together with the object, will be put together and shown to the class. Then each student will recite his or her piece of writing.

Niagara, Niagara

White mist

Endless thunder

Niagara, Niagara

Moving picture

Rolling power

5. Finally, both the object and the written representation will be exhibited on a table for creative student work, to be viewed by all the students.

Curriculum Connections

This strategy may be connected with learning a literary style or genre in English language arts and English literature classes. In addition, the strategy may be used for personal and creative writing activities. To enhance students' understanding of the connection between textual and visual representations, the teacher may wrap up the strategy by helping students brainstorm and talk about the meanings often associated with certain objects or images, such as a picture of holidays and celebrations. These may be expressed through a variety of symbolic forms, such as colorful images, visual objects, and expressive words.

STRATEGY 29
Internet Traveler

This strategy provides opportunities for students to do Internet-based, focused research about a particular country (or city) in the world. Specifically, the students will look for relevant information about the country's (or city's) population, language(s) spoken, weather, geographic location, history, literature, art, education, sports, tourist attractions, or any other interesting aspects. In addition, different students will have opportunities to organize the information found and to share their findings with other students in the class.

ELA Standard: 7

Beginning Learners

1. The teacher may begin by explaining to the students that they need to find information that is interesting to them about a foreign country or city. (This may be linked with what they are interested in or to the context of a particular novel they are reading.)

2. As it is developmentally quite challenging for the beginning learners to handle all the print and online texts by themselves, the teacher needs to carefully plan and lead the students through the searches. Students may be paired for the searches.

3. The teacher may use a picture-based encyclopedia, videos, and other audiovisual materials. Also, multicultural literature and Internet-based resources may be used.

4. Finally, the teacher may ask students to use drawings, symbols, or any other creative form to respond to what they have studied and learned about a particular country or city.

Intermediate Learners

1. Repeat Steps 1–4.

2. The teacher may modify the above steps by focusing on a particular author or a theme related to the curriculum, such as the rain forest in Brazil or the Great Wall of China.

Advanced Learners

1. The teacher begins by explaining to the students that they need to find information that is informative and engaging about a foreign country or city. (This may be linked with the content of their social studies or with the context of a particular novel they are reading.) For example, possible choices may include countries (or cities) dealt with in the social studies texts or countries (cities) of personal interest, such as Argentina, Brazil, China, Denmark, Egypt, France, Greece, Haiti, India, Japan, Korea, etc.

2. The teacher divides the students into small groups of three or four students, based on their interest or choice. Each group conducts online searches, as well as uses ordinary reference books and resources. Possible Web sites may include the Web site of the particular country's embassy in the U.S., tourist Web sites, and general or specific cultural Web sites. Based on the information gathered, each group decides on important and interesting information to be introduced to the other students.

3. Each group may use a written text during the presentation, and choose a main presenter (the other two or three students will work as presenter assistants) to share the results of their search, using handouts, PowerPoint, audiovisual materials, or any creative form.

4. After each group's presentation, other students may ask a few questions regarding the particular country (or city). All members of each group need to be prepared to respond to the questions from the audience, so as to make each presentation as informative and interactive as possible.

5. The teacher may ask each group to complete a written report to summarize or further explain their findings. The teacher may edit the reports and combine them into a class project called Internet Traveler.

Curriculum Connections

This strategy has the potential for cross-curriculum connections. First of all, it may be used in social studies class to help the students look for relevant information for understanding a country (or city) more systematically. Second, by focusing on a particular author instead of a country (or city), this strategy may be modified for use in ELA or English literature classes. The hands-on experience of Internet-based research may also provide opportunities for the students to develop their media literacy, critical thinking, and research. In addition, the information gathered may serve as the material source for them to write a report or summary of their research.

Global Perspectives and Literacy Development: Understanding the World View

STRATEGY 30
Community and Conflict: Peaceful Problem Solving

Often, conflicts that occur in classrooms relate to misunderstandings and the desire for only one way, so it's important to define peace with the class and talk about peaceful resolution. Questions to encourage discussion are, what does it mean to be peaceful? What do peaceful people do? What do people who don't know about peace do? When have you seen people being peaceful? When have you seen people who are not peaceful? Why are some people peaceful? Why are some people not peaceful?

Teaching young people to peacefully resolve conflict is an important skill (Watson & Ecken, 2003). Using trade books as well as class games and discussions can develop habits of peaceful resolution. Using hypothetical situations in class followed by discussions is a useful way to begin.

ELA Standards: 1 and 4

Beginning Learners

Brad and Jamie both want to play with the same truck. What can we do to help them decide how they will play with the truck? Have them go to a private corner and peacefully decide by asking these questions:

1. Can we play with the truck together?

2. If yes, what will Brad do with the truck and what will Jamie do with the truck?

3. If no, how will Brad and Jamie decide who plays with the truck first?

4. Who played with the truck yesterday or a little while ago?

5. What can Brad or Jamie play with while waiting his turn for the truck?

6. Do you need help from the teacher?

7. How did it feel to decide to be peaceful?

8. How does it feel when you don't know how to decide to be peaceful?

Intermediate Learners

Dori wants to be in a different group during a language arts activity. She wants to be in CeCe's group, not Lara's group, while writing a class play. Solve the problem together using the steps and examples below.

1. Gather information:

   I was in CeCe's group before.
   CeCe's group has a lot of good ideas.
   I like CeCe.
   I am friends with only one person in Lara's group.

2. Possible solutions:

   Change groups—going into CeCe's group may not be an option.
   Get to know people in Lara's group.
   Lara's group can use your help.
   Work alone.

3. Solution, for now: Working alone is boring. I might be able to help Lara's group, but I really don't want to. I'll try to join the group, because I want to get to know more people in the class.

Advanced Learners

1. For the advanced students, creating conflict situations that might arise and allowing students to take conflicting roles begin to help students walk in others' shoes. When they take the three roles in a scene such as the one above, they may think of ways to peacefully resolve the issue at hand. So

in groups of three, students can act out each role. Then they can try to solve the problem by brainstorming possible peaceful resolutions.

It's fair . . .

Daquan: Jerry made a joke about my sneakers and the goal I kicked in the soccer game. So I called his brother a druggie and threw a book at the wall. That's fair!

Teacher: Jerry, why did you joke about Daquan's sneakers?

Jerry: He made fun of my shirt yesterday.

Teacher: Jerry, why did you make fun of Daquan's goal?

Jerry: Only dummies play soccer.

Teacher: Did you feel better about making fun?

Jerry: Yeah!

Teacher: How did you feel, Jerry, when Daquan called your brother a name?

Jerry: You don't talk about my family that way. I didn't hit him. I threw a book.

Teacher: True, but you talked about his sports ability and the clothes he wears. Is it fair to do that? Daquan, how did you feel about saying all that about Jerry's brother?

Daquan: Good, cuz he is a druggie!

---

2. So what is fair? How can this conflict be resolved and possibly prevent future confrontations?

Curriculum Connections

Reading, writing, listening, speaking, and viewing are all integrated for language arts activities that promote critical thinking. The skills used are life skills that may have a great impact on student thinking in all content areas, particularly social studies. We claim that we study history to learn from the past. Peaceful resolution has implications for family, community, and country.

Teachers' Comments

"I think this strategy translates to classroom practice, but I'm not sure about when they leave."

"I'd like to see if they can make the leap to our nation and world dealings."

"I like the class discussions. Students begin to think about real alternatives."

STRATEGY 31
Being Grateful for Diversity

Our world is a planet with many species of plant and animal life. Much of the life on the planet depends on other life for survival. Therefore, we should be grateful and protective of this world. Diverse groups of people demonstrate such thanksgiving for the world in many different ways. The purpose of this strategy is to help students see not only the many differences in our world but also the many ways people give thanks for the differences around them. The following literature stimulates conversations about world diversity and may help the class begin a search for the ways that different people give thanks for the diversity in our world.

- Spier, P., *People*
- Bunting, E., *Terrible Things*
- Cherry, L., *A River Runs Wild*
- Cherry, L., & Plotkin, M., *The Shaman's Apprentice*
- Cherry, L., *The Great Kapok Tree*

ELA Standard: 9

Beginning Learners

1. Read one of the stories and talk about the beautiful people, plants, and animals in the story.

2. Ask the students to talk about the same around their homes and schools.

3. Take a walk around the school and talk about the people, plants, and animals seen.

4. When the students return to the classroom, record all on chart paper.

5. Categorize on chart paper . . . teachers, principals, third grade, indoor plants, fifth grade, custodians, etc.

6. Ask the students to look at all the people, plant, and animal differences they saw. "What would happen if one of the groups or categories went away?"

7. Students draw two pictures of a particular part of the school they visited, such as the third-grade class or the principal's office, or the playground—one with the group missing and one with the group present, e.g., playground with no grass . . . a class with no teacher . . . a teacher with no class . . . a room with no indoor plants or aquarium.

8. Create a bulletin board showing all the living things we need in our world. Title the board "We are thankful for the living things around us."

9. Invite a Native American or an ecologist to talk about our world and why we need to take care of it.

Intermediate Learners

1. Invite visitors from different cultures or family members and ask them to talk about how they show they are grateful for the world around them.

2. Students record the many ways people give thanks for living things. For instance, they may talk about taking care of their yards and pets; recycling trash; planting flowers, trees, or vegetables; cleaning their homes; driving safe cars; wearing a helmet, or obeying the law.

3. Search the Internet in pairs or threes to discover how other people in other lands give thanks for the world's living things. How do they say "Thank you for the world" in other languages?

WE ARE THANKFUL

How do people from Beijing give thanks for their world?

How do people from Tokyo give thanks for their world?

How do people from Mexico City give thanks for their world?

How do people from the United States give thanks for their world?

How do people from Germany give thanks for their world?

How do people from Israel give thanks for their world?

How do people from Nigeria give thanks for their world?

How do people from Tanzania give thanks for their world?

How do people from the Sudan give thanks for their world?

How do people from Syria give thanks for their world?

How do people from India give thanks for their world?

How do people from Russia give thanks for their world?

How do people from Samoa give thanks for their world?

How do people from Australia give thanks for their world?

Advanced Learners

1. Follow steps for the intermediate level, but add more in-depth searches using terms such as biodiversity, ecology, United Nations, balance of nature, and Kyoto Treaty.

2. Students in pairs select one country to research in order to discover how the people are preserving their environment and biodiversity.

3. Visit a recycling plant to discover what is happening in the community to preserve the environment.

4. Begin a recycling program in the school.

Curriculum Connections

All content areas are included in this strategy. Numerous aspects of biodiversity relate to social studies, science, statistics, and language arts. Thematic instruction is ideal. This may occur in one classroom or several classrooms. It might even be the year's theme involving all grade levels.

Teachers' Comments

"This strategy teaches about the big picture. My students enjoyed it."
"This brought a new dimension to my classes. I liked it."
"We can't teach religion, but we can teach respect and responsibility."

STRATEGY 32
The World and Our Place in It

This strategy aims at promoting students' environmental and geographical awareness as an aspect of diversity. Through studying maps of the world, the U.S., the state, and the city or town, students have opportunities to develop an understanding of their "geographical locality," as well as a global perspective about the interconnectedness between any individual and the natural world we all live in.

ELA Standard: 7

Beginning Learners

1. The teacher may begin by explaining that the world we live in is like a huge ball. Using a globe, the teacher points out the major continents and oceans, i.e., Africa, Asia, Europe, Oceania, North and South America, the Antarctic, the Atlantic, the Pacific, the Indian Ocean, and the Arctic Ocean.

2. The teacher hangs up maps of the world, the U.S., the state, and the city in which the school is located, side by side.

3. On the world map, the teacher points out the location of the U.S. in North America, then moves on to the U.S. map of the 50 states (emphasizing the specific state in which the students live). The teacher then moves on to the state map to point out the different counties and cities within the state, emphasizing the city or town in which the students live.

4. The teacher points out the major streets and roads, landmarks, and the location of the school, adding that it is in this school building in a particular classroom where they are studying the maps.

5. Now working through all the maps backwards, i.e., from the city or town map to the world map, the teacher traces the locality of the school in relation to the city or town, the state, the U.S., and the world, emphasizing the connectedness of the specific locality to the larger world.

6. Students draw a picture of their homes and the roads where they live.

Intermediate Learners

1. Repeat Steps 1–6.

2. The teacher asks the students to draw a rough map of the major roads and streets between each student's home and the school.

3. Using a state or U.S. map, students point out the places that they have lived in or visited (or would like to visit).

4. The students work to locate important cities and landmarks on the U.S. map, such as Washington, D.C., New York City, Chicago, Los Angeles, the Grand Canyon, Lake Erie, etc.

Advanced Learners

1. Repeat the above Steps 1–4.

2. The students write an essay about the places they have studied in their coursework, have visited, or would like to visit.

3. The teacher explains the concept of *scale* in mapmaking. The teacher divides the students into groups of three. Each group will measure on the maps the distance between, or the size of, the states, the cities, or towns they are interested in. Then they calculate the rough distances or sizes of these places in terms of miles or square miles.

Curriculum Connections

This strategy may be used in social studies class. It is particularly relevant when the class is working on the geography of the world, the U.S., and the state in which students live. This strategy may also be used in math class, as shown in Step 3 with the advanced learners. Additionally, students may write an essay on what they have learned about environmental and geographical diversity.

STRATEGY 33
Diverse Means of Transportation

This strategy provides opportunities for students to learn the various means of transportation across regions and countries. Students will learn that, besides private cars, people use buses, subways, trains, planes, boats, motorcycles, and bicycles, as well as just walking to get to places. This strategy helps young learners be aware of the diverse means of transportation, as one important aspect of the diverse and colorful cultures and lifestyles across countries and regions.

ELA Standard: 7

Beginning Learners

1. The teacher may begin by asking how the students come to school or go shopping with their parents. Then, the teacher explains that not all children go to school by school bus or go shopping by car. For example, children in rural Kenya walk to school, people in China often ride bicycles to work, and some people in Vietnam take boat rides to go places.

2. The teacher shows pictures or flash cards of various means of transportation, such as car, bus, subway, train, plane, boat, motorcycle, bicycle, etc. While showing the pictures or cards, the teacher also writes the names of the vehicles on the board for the students to see.

3. The teacher helps the students brainstorm about different means of transportation. For example, drive a car for grocery shopping, take the train or fly for long-distance trips, or take a boat when visiting the Caribbean, etc. The teacher may explain that the choice of the means of transportation often has to do with the convenience, expense, and time involved.

4. The teacher asks the students to consider the means of travel from the U.S. to an African, Asian, or European country, emphasizing that the early immigrants to the U.S. came from all over the world by boats across the Atlantic or Pacific, but nowadays people fly.

Intermediate Learners

1. Repeat Steps 1–4.

2. The teacher divides the students into small groups of three or four to study the various aspects related to different means of transportation, such as the history related to trains, subways, boats, planes, cars, buses, etc. Each group selects a topic they would like to explore further by gathering informative and interesting facts from books, encyclopedias, or online resources.

3. Each group shares their findings with the other students through a 3- to 5-minute group presentation.

Advanced Learners

1. Repeat the above Steps 1–3.

2. Possible topics for students to explore in study groups of three may include the numbers of cars owned or other means of transportation used in a particular country, or inventors or engineers who made significant contributions to the advancement of the varied means of transportation.

3. Each group prepares a written report about their findings.

4. The teacher and the students edit and combine the reports into a class project called Transportation and Our Lives.

Curriculum Connections

This strategy may be used in the social studies and geography classes to help the students to better understand the various means of transportation used across regions and countries. While the strategy helps students develop their general awareness of the diverse means of transportation used across regions and countries, the presentation and written report help them develop their oral communication and writing skills.

STRATEGY 34
Compassion: Journal Writing, Interviewing, and Theatrical Presentation

Helping a student walk in the shoes of another person is basic to human understanding and appreciation. With the study of compassion taking place on a daily basis in the classroom and school, the problems related to bullying may subside, and an appreciation for differences may become the norm.

ELA Standards: 1 and 4

Beginning Learners

1. Read stories like *Reach for the Sky* (1999), by Stoutland, that specifically talk about caring and sharing and thinking of how others feel. Students can relate the book to their own world, giving them the tools they need to become compassionate human beings.

2. *Manners* by Aliki can be read and then students can think of similar situations at home and school. They can then recreate the situations in small groups and present to the rest of the class.

3. Interviewing is a way to discover likes and dislikes. Students sit in pairs facing each other. The teacher models an interview with a student, asking a couple of questions. Then the student interviews the other student asking the same questions, such as, "What is your favorite book? Why?" or "What is your favorite dessert? Why?" When the interview is complete, everyone reports to the whole class about what they learned. The teacher records the information on chart paper. Students then pretend they are the people they interviewed and they draw/write in a journal. Below is an example.

Intermediate Learners

1. Visitors from the school and community come to class to be interviewed. Students write a journal concerning a day in the person's life.

2. Students interview people outside the school . . . minister, nurse, teacher, plumber, cook, law officer, etc. They find out about the day of the interviewee and write "A Day in the Life" for that person. Students may create the interview questions. The following is a sample:

(Possible) Interview—not necessary to ask all questions

- What is your name?
- Why were you given that name?
- Tell about a memory before you came to school. Why do you remember it?
- How many brothers and sisters do you have?

- What's your favorite holiday? Why?
- What's your favorite food? Why?
- What's your favorite sport? Why?
- What's your favorite place? Why?
- What's your favorite TV show? Why?
- What are your favorite things to do? Why?
- Tell about the best time in your life.
- Tell me about your day from the time you wake up to the time you go to sleep.

After the interview, the student recreates a day in the life of the person from that person's perspective.

Suzie's Day

I got up this morning and put on the pink jeans. I fed my dog, Muffy. I love Muffy. I did not eat breakfast. I go to school. I am happy. I like my friends in school. I do not like to play outside. I get very hungry for lunch.

I play in the drama center. I like riding the bus home to my Grandma's house. Mother gets me and takes me home to watch TV. We have ice cream for dessert. I do my homework. Yuk! Mother reads to me and I read to her. Then I go to sleep. Good Night!

Advanced Learners

The previous ideas may be used, but additionally, literature relating to tragic figures may be the focus of journal writing, interviewing, and theatrical re-creation. In these books, the characters deal with issues that young people in different times and places have had to deal with. Their struggles may be similar to present day studies. Therefore, compassion can easily be the focus.

- Creech, S. (1994). *Walk Two Moons*—Social Studies, English, Science, Mathematics
- Flake, S. (1999). *The Skin I'm In*—Social Studies, English
- Fox, P. (1991). *Monkey Island*—Social Studies, English, Science
- Konisburg, E. I. (1997). *A View From Saturday*—Social Studies
- Lowry, L. (1993). *The Giver*—Science, Math
- Speare, E. G. (1958). *Witch of Blackbird Pond*—Social Studies, Math, Science, English
- Yep, L. (1975). *Dragonwings*—Social Studies, Math, Science, English, Art
- Yolen, J. (1990). *The Devil's Arithmetic*—Math, Social Studies, Science, English

Curriculum Connections

Language arts is the focus, but careers of visitors and interviewees relate to the content areas. Additionally, the young adult literature is linked to content areas for thematic instruction if teachers decide to collaborate.

Teachers' Comments

"My students got into this! They worked so well together on these projects."

"I did this at the beginning of the school year and my classes were so much better this year."

"I just like doing this. It covers most of the ELA standards and promotes character education."

STRATEGY 35
Weather and Us

Weather includes all the changes in temperature, wind, and air pressure. It affects everyone in the world: we may feel hot or cold; it may be windy or foggy; sometimes there is too much rain or snow. Because it is a natural phenomenon, we may predict possible weather, but cannot do much to change it. As weather patterns change from region to region, awareness of different kinds of weather activities across regions and seasons may present another kind of diversity to the young students. This strategy provides opportunities for the students to be aware of a variety of weather activities. As a result, students will not only learn the vocabulary for different weather phenomena, but also get to understand the impact of weather on human lives. In addition, the teacher may divide the students into small study groups to further explore the secrets of an extraordinary type of weather, such as a hurricane, tornado, or blizzard.

ELA Standard: 7

Beginning Learners

1. The teacher may begin by explaining that the air movement influenced by the sun (and other stars in space) causes wind, rain, or snow on the Earth, and different weather patterns affect human lives differently. For example, snow makes the road slippery, and people need to be careful while walking or driving.

2. The teacher uses pictures or flash cards to illustrate various kinds of wind: breeze, gust, hurricane, tornado, typhoon, zephyr, draft, squall, cyclone, etc. While explaining the different kinds of wind, the teacher writes down these words on the board for the students to see.

3. Similarly, the teacher illustrates weather words about snow or rain, such as snow shower, sleet, snowstorm, blizzard, whiteout, flurry, lake effect snow, nor'easter, ice storm, snow pellet or rain shower, downpour, drizzle, rainstorm, cloudburst, thunderstorm, cloudburst, hail, torrential rain, etc.

4. The teacher brainstorms with the students about what kind of weather each student likes or dislikes. The teacher explains that people living in different geographic regions generally have different weather, and thus different experiences with the weather.

5. The teacher encourages the students to share their unusual experiences with extraordinary weather.

Intermediate Learners

1. Repeat Steps 1–5.

2. The teacher asks the students to brainstorm in small groups about the weather and the four seasons, and link typical weather with different geographical regions in the U.S. and in the world.

3. Students in groups brainstorm ideas, design clothing for the four seasons, and share with the class.

Advanced Learners

1. Repeat the above Steps 1–3.

2. The teacher divides the students into small study groups of three or four and asks each group to select a particular kind of weather (e.g., hurricane, ice storm, etc.). Each group will study the causes and conditions for certain weather activity, using information from geography and weather encyclopedias, or online resources.

3. Each group prepares a 10-minute presentation of their findings about the weather they have studied, using drawings, models, PowerPoint, or any other creative form. After each group's presentation, other students may ask a few questions.

4. Each group prepares a written summary of the particular type of weather they have studied.

5. The teacher edits the summaries written by different groups and combines them into a class project called Weather and Us.

6. Invite a meteorologist to the class and interview him or her.

Curriculum Connections

This strategy may be used in geography class. While it is useful to teach all students to understand diverse weather phenomena in the U.S. and around the world, the strategy is particularly suitable for students to study the salient weather in their own region. In addition, the strategy is useful in developing students' abilities to read and understand informational texts related to the weather.

STRATEGY 36
Speaking and Learning Languages

Our nation developed as a place for those who were forced to leave their home countries due to economic, political, and social reasons. Many came out of fear, but with the hope for better and safer lives. Some believed it was their only chance for survival. As a result, they brought their languages and cultures to our shores. Their contributions often enriched the lives of the many who were already established. However, their struggles to reconcile their own cultures with the existing cultures often caused great conflicts and hardships. Thankfully, many of their contributions have survived, and made our country the unique blend of which we are so proud. In the process, though, many languages and cultural traditions were lost and this caused irreparable emotional damage. We now understand the benefits of assisting the new people in our land. Teachers are beginning to make use of some simple ways of validating the experiences of students from other lands as a means of enriching all student learning. When teachers implement these ideas, these immigrant students will adjust more rapidly and learn the English language and American culture without experiencing negative feelings related to diminishing their home languages and cultures.

ELA Standard: 10

The following ideas create classroom learning environments that celebrate languages in grades K–8 (Cazden, 2001; Cummins, 1986; Igoa, 1995; Schmidt, 1998c).

1. Label objects in the classroom two or three languages, such as desk, chair, book, teacher, students, etc. Have the student and/or family member assist the teacher if necessary. Labeling is common in primary classrooms. It works great in secondary classrooms too. A daily practice pronouncing the vocabulary highlights other cultures and languages. This small amount of time recognizes differences and teaches everyone in the class a second language.

2. Invite students/family members to present information or artifacts from the country of origin. For example, many Southeast Asian students have jewelry and art objects they can share.

3. Use paired learning.

4. Give opportunities for students to speak, read, or write in the home language each day in school.

5. Include visuals wherever and whenever possible, such as videos, overhead transparencies, photos from disposable cameras, and posters, when teaching.

6. Implement hands-on classroom experiences and field trips.

7. Post the daily class schedule or schedule of the day. This creates a predictable environment for learning.

8. Hang a map of the world or display a globe.

9. Make use of choral reading.

10. Make dictionaries available—English to Spanish; English to Mandarin.

11. Use nonfiction picture books to teach key concepts in content areas.

12. Include the culture—e.g., famous Latino chemists, famous Chinese artists.

13. Encourage drawing/writing.

14. Have students keep a personal journal.

15. Help the students keep an assignment pad.

Curriculum Connections

The above ideas are basic to all classrooms and content areas K–8. A kindergartener may not be able to use a dictionary, but he or she could create an English-Spanish dictionary using pictures from a magazine or drawings and inventive spelling. A kindergarten student may memorize a song or nursery rhyme and could help a Vietnamese student learn the words as part of a choral reading experience. Many of the activities are used with students who have special learning needs, and most of the ideas presented make learning a more positive and integrated experience for all students. Accommodations are often examples of "just plain good teaching."

Teachers' Comments

"I found this strategy offered me some real ways to work with ELL students."
"These ideas are so positive for the students in the class."
"If I just follow these ideas, I will make a big difference for my ELL students and my regular students."

STRATEGY 37
Flora and Fauna of Regions

Flora refers to the plant life of a certain region of the world whereas fauna refers to the animal life of a certain region or time. This strategy provides opportunities for students to develop an awareness (and an appreciation) of the colorful and diverse plant and animal life across various geographical regions. We humans are not the only beings living on the Earth, and there is a rich world full of all kinds of life forms around us. In addition, students will have an opportunity to learn the unique state flower or animal, or the flower or animal of a particular country in the world.

ELA Standard: 7

Beginning Learners

1. The teacher may begin by asking the students to name the symbolic flower and animal of their state. Then, the teacher shares with them about the symbolic flowers and animals of the 50 U.S. states. For example, in Illinois, the official state bird is the northern cardinal, the official state animal the white-tailed deer, the official state tree the white oak, the official state fish the bluegill, the official state insect the monarch butterfly, and the official state flower the violet.

2. The teacher asks the students to tell their favorite flower, plant, or animal.

3. The teacher shows pictures or stories of some unique plants and animals living in different natural habitats, such as the oceans, the rivers, the rain forests, the deserts, the Arctic, the Antarctic, Africa, Asia, Australia, South and North America, etc.

4. The teacher explains that flora and fauna, like many other things in the world, are diverse across geographic regions. It is these various forms of diversity that make the world, and our lives in the world, colorful and interesting.

5. Take a field trip on a nature trail. After returning to the classroom, students create a mural depicting diverse flora and fauna seen on the nature trail.

Intermediate Learners

1. Repeat Steps 1–5.

2. The teacher asks the students to identify some flora and fauna that are found only in certain regions. For example, kangaroos are found only in central Australia, giant pandas are only found in central China, toco toucans are only found in eastern South America, and huon pines are found only in western and southern Tasmania.

3. Each student studies a special plant or animal that he or she is interested in, using picture books, photos, drawings, a children's encyclopedia, etc.

4. The teacher invites volunteers to share with the class any information they have gathered about the plant and animal they have studied.

Advanced Learners

1. Repeat the above Steps 1–4.

2. The teacher divides the students into small study groups of three to four. Each group will select some unique animal or plant to study further, drawing from personal experiences, books, a children's encyclopedia, online resources, etc. They make a 10-minute presentation to share their findings with the other students.

3. Each group prepares a written report summarizing the major findings.

4. The teacher edits the reports from different groups and combines them into a class project called Flora and Fauna Around the World.

Curriculum Connections

This strategy may be used in social studies, geography, and biology classes to help the students better understand the diversity of flora and fauna around the world and in the students' particular state or region. The group project may help the students read and understand informational texts. Additionally, the presentation and the written report may help their oral communication skills and writing skills.

STRATEGY 38
Architecture Around the World

This strategy aims to develop the students' awareness of architectural diversity in the world. Housing, along with food, clothing, and transportation, has traditionally been a basic necessity for human survival. Through this strategy, students may be helped to become aware of the various architectural styles associated with different historical periods, cultures, or regions, as a reflection of the people's culture, history, or lifestyle.

ELA Standard: 7

Beginning and Intermediate Learners

1. The teacher may begin by showing some pictures or video clips about scenes from around the world, such as churches, temples, mosques, skyscrapers, flat roofs, cave dwellings, brick buildings, wooden houses, etc. These may include some historic or culturally symbolic sites, such as the White House, the Golden Gate Bridge, the Great Wall, the Great Pyramid, St. Peter's Cathedral, the Holy Mosque in Mecca, etc.

2. The teacher and students brainstorm architectural differences they might find in various places in the U.S., such as in a rural area, in the city, or in the suburbs, explaining that in the city they are likely to find more high-rise buildings, farmers in the country would build barns for crops or livestock, and in the suburbs there are more neighborhoods with separate houses.

3. The teacher explains that in different regions in the world, people build different kinds of buildings due to considerations such as the environment, historical or cultural influences, natural materials for construction, and technological equipment and know-how. For example, in areas with frequent earthquakes, buildings are often low; in snowy regions houses tend to have steep roofs; in some Asian countries there are not many wooden houses because timber and energy are not as abundant as they are in North America, etc.

4. The beginning learners may talk about their ideas when seeing the different buildings. The intermediate learners may write a short essay about what they have learned from viewing and examining the various architectural styles.

Advanced Learners

1. Repeat the above Steps 1–4.

2. The students get into small groups of three or four. Each group selects a culturally symbolic building, or a historical style of building to study, using travel books, photos, video clips, a children's encyclopedia, or online resources.

3. Each group gives a 10-minute presentation of their findings to the whole class.

4. Each group prepares a written report of their major findings.

5. The teacher edits and combines the reports into a class project called Architectural Diversity in the World.

Curriculum Connections

This strategy may be used in social studies and geography classes to help the students understand that architecture is yet another aspect of human cultural diversity. The strategy may be used in art and social studies classes. The presentation and written report are useful in helping the students' oral and written English skills.

STRATEGY 39
Calendar of Holidays/Festivals From Around the World

Students gather information from different countries/cultures about their important cultural traditions, customs, or celebrations. The purpose of this strategy is to enhance students' multicultural awareness and knowledge of other cultural practices and customs. Based on the information gathered by all the students, the teacher may facilitate as students complete a class project by creating a multicultural calendar that includes all major holidays and festivals from the world.

ELA Standards: 4 and 7

Beginning Learners

1. For beginning learners, the teacher may begin by helping the students identify major holidays they are familiar with. For example, Christmas, Thanksgiving, Easter, Halloween, Labor Day, Independence Day, Veteran's Day, Valentine's Day, and Mother's Day.

2. Teacher and students talk about the histories and celebrations that go together with each holiday and festival. While entering dates in the calendar, the teacher may encourage students to wonder about how people in other countries celebrate their own holidays and festivals.

3. The teacher then reads books, shows videos, or uses other cultural artifacts (e.g., a small lantern to talk about the Chinese Lantern Festival) to introduce different countries' holidays and festivals.

4. As more information is provided to students, the teacher may help them identify the relevant dates and celebrations.

5. After they enter the dates in the big calendar, they have created their cultural calendar.

Intermediate Learners

1. Repeat Steps 1–5.

2. The teacher may modify the above steps for the beginning learners by allowing for more student involvement in the process of creating the multicultural calendar.

Advanced Learners

1. Based on the number of students, the class will come up with a list of the same number of countries to be studied. The teacher makes sure to include all countries to which students in the class are ethnically, culturally, or linguistically related. Ask each student to represent a particular country.

2. Each student's responsibility is to search on the Internet, read books, watch videos, or talk to knowledgeable individuals about some of the important holidays and festivals for the particular country that he or she studies.

3. Each student will present the dates, origins, celebrations, or customs associated with at least five holidays and festivals for each country. Then, he or she will prepare a written report about the relevant information for the larger class project.

4. After all students have finished their reports, the teacher will prepare a big monthly calendar for entering the relevant dates and important celebrations of the different holidays and festivals, creating a cultural calendar as a class project.

5. After the cultural calendar has been created, the teacher may refer back to the calendar and reiterate those important cultural dates and celebrations. The written reports may be used to provide more specific information about each holiday and festival.

Curriculum Connections

This strategy may be linked with social studies and geography courses. To promote acceptance and tolerance among students, the teacher may deliberately choose to include those countries and cultures that are related to students from diverse ethnic and cultural backgrounds, but which are unknown to other students in the class.

STRATEGY 40
Differences in Names and in Addresses

This strategy involves different ways of writing names and postal addresses. When writing an address in English, it is normal to begin with the individual recipient's name (first name first, then last name), and move on to the house number, the street, the city, the state/province, and the zip code. When it is international mail, the name of the country is also needed, at the end. In certain cultures, however, the ways a name is formed and an address is written are entirely different. This strategy teaches students a different way of viewing names and writing postal addresses practiced in other cultures.

ELA Standard: 6

Beginning and Intermediate Learners

1. The teacher explains first name and last name explicitly. For example, with *Matt Smith*, the first name is Matt, and the last name is Smith.

2. The teacher helps students better understand the general conventions of writing a postal address by asking each student to copy his or her family's address. They then read their addresses and compare and contrast similarities and differences. Last, each writes a note or draws a picture for a friend or family member. Each addresses an envelope and the class as a group mails them at the school postal drop.

Advanced Learners

1. The teacher may begin by calling a few students' full names to explain how a postal address is written. The teacher may also show the envelope of an actual letter, written in English. The teacher may explain that a name in the United States is made up of the first name and the last name, which form the first line of the postal address. Then it is house, street, city, and state, followed by the zip code.

2. Next, the teacher explains that not all names and addresses are written this way. For example, in China, Japan, and Korea, one's last (family) name appears before his or her first (given) name. In the Disney children's movie *Mulan*, the full name of the heroine is Hua Mulan, in which Hua is her last (family) name, and Mulan is her first (given) name.

3. If a letter was written in Chinese, Japanese, or Korean, the actual order of the address would be the opposite of what is written in English. It would begin with the state/province and move on to the city, the street, the house number, and the recipient's name (last name first, then first name).

4. The teacher may encourage the students to brainstorm about the cultural meaning of these differences. For instance, culturally, Hua

Mulan's full name means that Mulan is a member within the Hua family. Also, culturally, it suggests that "me" (or any individual) is not the starting point in the world. Instead, the individual is located within the context of the "big picture" or the world to begin with the "big picture" in which the individual is located, and then is scaled down.

5. The teacher may also explain that names and addresses are just two examples that show different perspectives on the relationships between one and his or her family and between one and his or her larger environment. With people coming from different ethnic and cultural backgrounds in the U.S., it is therefore important to be sensitive to different perspectives on issues in cross-cultural communication.

Curriculum Connections

Literacy learning may be facilitated with a variety of language usage for authentic communication. By examining the differences in names and addresses in other cultures, students will enhance their awareness of multicultural practices and different perspectives embedded within similar practices.

STRATEGY 41
Group Poems

This strategy provides opportunities for the students to compose a poem as a group on a theme that is close to their lives and interests. By asking each student to contribute a line (or two) of a poem, the teacher creates a fun and collective atmosphere for composing and appreciating poems. With ESL learners who are in the beginning stages of English acquisition, it may be necessary for the teacher to provide assistance, or pair them with an English speaker.

ELA Standard: 6

Beginning Learners

1. The teacher may begin by explaining how a group poem is composed. An example, might be entitled *My Cat*, as shown below:

First Student:	*My cat has stripes of brown and yellow.*
Second Student:	*She loves to lick her soft furry coat.*
Third Student:	*Sometimes she acts so very mellow.*
Fourth Student:	*Sometimes she purrs deep down in her throat.*

2. The teacher then provides a list of topics as possible themes for composing a group poem (or a lyric story with beginning learners). The topics need to be quite specific things familiar to the children, such as "my dog," "walking in the rain," "a favorite song," etc.

3. After the teacher and the class decide on a particular topic, each student needs to think and come up with a line that is related to the theme and appropriate in the context so all the lines form a group poem. While the students are working on the poem orally, the teacher facilitates the composing process by calling students to contribute and writes down every line supplied by the students.

4. After the poem is completed, the teacher and the class revise and edit the poem to make it coherent and cohesive. The class recites the final version of the poem chorally.

Intermediate Learners

1. Repeat Steps 1–3.

2. In addition to the specific topics mentioned above, broader topics, as well as books read by the class may be included. For example, "Unforgettable Friendship," reading "Tuck Everlasting," "By the Lake," etc.

3. Instead of composing a class poem, the teacher may also divide the students into groups of four to compose a poem on a topic they choose.

Advanced Learners

1. Repeat the above Steps 1–3.

2. Besides orally composing the poem, each group may write down their lines and hand in the "finished" poem to the teacher as a polished, written product. The students may also add drawings or other artistic forms to enhance their poem.

3. The teacher may edit all the group poems and combine them into a class project called Our Group Poem.

Curriculum Connections

Poem study is an interesting but often weak area of study for many students. By employing group poem composition as an alternative strategy to the traditional methods in teaching and writing poems in ELA and English literature classes, the teacher may create a more relaxed and enjoyable way for students to learn and to appreciate poems.

TOURO COLLEGE LIBRARY

STRATEGY 42
Recipe Books

This strategy aims at helping students develop awareness and appreciation of the different culinary traditions and practices from around the world. The diversity in foods found in the U.S. is a living reminder of the colorful diversity among the peoples and the cultures of the U.S. Students may come to understand that the foods, like many other aspects of the culture, were brought to the U.S. by diverse groups of people from varied places. These groups simultaneously to maintain the original flavors and adapt to American tastes.

ELA Standard: 7

Beginning Learners

1. The teacher may begin by asking each student to tell his or her favorite food, which the teacher will write on the board.

2. The teacher leads the class to examine the origins of some of the foods mentioned by the students. For example, pizza came from Naples, Italy; hamburgers came from Hamburg, Germany; nachos came from Mexico; dumplings came from China, etc.

3. The teacher may explain the differences between an ordinary restaurant and a fast food restaurant, emphasizing the risks of putting on weight as a result of eating too much fast food.

4. The teacher then asks student volunteers to bring in a variety of foods from home for a food appreciation festival.

Intermediate Learners

1. Repeat Steps 1–4.

2. The teacher asks each student to ask the parents or grandparents, or search online, for the recipe for making a particular kind of food or drink.

3. With help from family members, students prepare food samples to be shared in class.

Advanced Learners

1. Repeat the above Steps 1–3.

2. Each student writes a report about the recipe for his or her favorite food(s), with the recipe included in the report.

3. The teacher edits and combines all the recipes to make a Recipe Book as a class project.

Curriculum Connections

This strategy can be used with the social studies classes. While students may develop a keener sense of the great variety of foods in the U.S., they may also learn to appreciate the food culture, together with other contributions, of a particular people dealt with in their lessons. Additionally, the strategy may be useful in teaching the vocabulary for food items, and students may develop an appreciation of the foods their families make and enjoy.

STRATEGY 43
Converting From the
U.S. System to the Metric System

This strategy aims at helping students develop an awareness of the different systems to quantify things (e.g., distance, temperature, and weight). It also introduces some basic knowledge about the metric system that is being used in most countries in the world today. For example, students who are familiar with miles (or feet or inches) may learn to use kilometers (or meters or centimeters) for measuring distance, or vice versa. The purpose of this is, in general, to teach students different systems of measurement used in different countries, and specifically to teach the differences and similarities of the metric and the U.S. systems for measuring distance.

ELA Standards: 4 and 7

Beginning Learners

1. The teacher may begin by asking students about the different speed limits on highways, county roads, residential streets, or school streets. After writing down the varied speed limits in terms of miles per hour, the teacher asks the students how long 1 mile is.

2. The teacher then introduces the concept of foot, using a wooden yardstick for the students to see the actual length. A foot is a unit of length used in the U.S. and Britain, equal to 12 inches or 1/3 of a yard; 5,280 feet make up 1 mile.

3. The teacher then explains that in Canada (and in other countries where people use the metric system), driving speed is expressed in terms of kilometers per hour. For example, the speed limits may be 100, 50, or 30 kilometers per hour on different roads.

4. The teacher proceeds to introduce the concept of meter, again using a wooden meter stick for students to see the actual length. A meter is a unit of length used in the international metric system; 1,000 meters make up one kilometer; one meter equals 100 centimeters.

5. Students, in pairs, measure each other using meter sticks and yardsticks.

Intermediate Learners

1. Repeat Steps 1–5.

2. The teacher then provides the following two equations for converting between the U.S. and the metric systems: 1 mile = 5,280 feet = 1.852 kilometers = 1,852 meters; 1 kilometer = 1,000 meters = 0.621 mile = 3,281 feet.

3. To practice with these units of measurement, the teacher divides the class into pairs. One of the two students will use the meter stick, and

the other student will use the yardstick to actually measure the size of the classroom, the bookshelf, the desk, or other objects in the classroom. Afterwards, each student's task is to convert the numbers they have obtained to the other system of measure, i.e., from U.S. to metric, or from metric to U.S.

Objects	Centimeters	Inches
Classroom Floor		
Bookshelf		
Desk		
Dictionary		
Chair		
. . . . . .		

Advanced Learners

1. Repeat Steps 1–3.

2. The teacher uses the following problem to wrap up the work on this strategy. John and Mary traveled to another country by taking an international flight. They had a suitcase of $3 \times 4 \times 5$ feet, and the airline's maximum size for luggage was $1 \times 1.2 \times 1.5$ meters. Do you think they were allowed to take their suitcase on the flight? Why or why not? After they arrived, they rented a car to drive around. The local speed limit was 80 kilometers per hour. John thought that speed limit was equal to 60 miles per hour, and Mary insisted it would be 50 miles per hour. Who do you think was right? Why?

3. In addition, the teacher may replace the example of distance with temperature, involving the Fahrenheit (F) scale and the Celsius scale (C) to indicate temperature, using the equation: $F = 1.8C + 32$. The teacher may also use the example of weight expressed by the U.S. and the metric systems, using the equation: 1 pound = 0. 45359 kilogram = 453.59 grams.

Curriculum Connections

This strategy may be useful for teaching math and science classes. The students may learn the differences and similarities of the U.S. and the metric systems by using the equations provided; learning scientific concepts; and performing addition, subtraction, and simple multiplication. Moreover, the hands-on experiences embedded in measuring the size, temperature, or weight of things can enhance students' awareness for diverse perspectives to view and measure things in the world.

6

Inquiry Learning and Literacy Learning: Beginning to Know Research

STRATEGY 44
KWLQ: Researching Diversity

Based on the work of Donna Ogle's (1986) KWL, KWLQ (Schmidt, 1999a) helps students begin to do research successfully. Students learn to study by using a stragety that organizes thinking and systematically takes students through an inquiry learning process. First, students record "K," what they know about a topic. Next is "W," where the students list questions that will help them learn about the topic. They begin to read, skim, and study information related to the topic, and also interview experts, watch videos, and/or take field trips to find answers outside of texts. Then students record answers to their questions under "L" as well as any other information learned in their search. Finally, "Q" is the place where they record more questions . . . excellent research should end with more questions for further study. Students learn that research is not a linear process, but an ever evolving process of inquiry.

ELA Standard: 5 and 7

Beginning Learners

1. On a chart marked with "K, What I Know" the teacher records what students know about skin color and other differences we see in the people we know. This might take several days.

2. Students, using a mirror and multicultural crayons, paint or draw their own faces with felt-tip markers. These are shared with the class and similarities and differences are discussed.

3. On a chart marked with "W, What I Want to Know" about differences we see in the people we know, the teacher records questions students have about differences.

4. Next, students are read books, see videos, and receive visitors from different ethnic and cultural groups.

5. After these events, students, with the teacher facilitating, answer the questions on the chart labeled "L, What I learned." They also add learned information other than answers to the questions.

6. Finally, the "Q, More Questions" is the last chart. The students list more questions they have about people's differences.

Intermediate and Advanced Learners

1. Students are given a KWLQ chart and discuss the meaning of it. In pairs, they fill in the first box concerning what they know about human differences.

What I **K**now	**W**hat I Want to Know
What I **L**earned	More **Q**uestions

2. Students, in pairs, draw with pencil and multicultural crayons each other's faces while talking about various features and skin tones. The portraits, as well as each pair's process, are shared in class.

3. A video or an illustrated story concerning human differences is presented and discussed in order to build students' background knowledge concerning human differences. (School librarians and the Internet can be invaluable sources for excellent materials.)

4. In pairs, students write questions concerning what they want to know about human differences in the W of the chart. These are shared with the whole class, and the teacher places the questions on a class chart.

5. Visitors to class from different ethnic and cultural backgrounds may come to talk about their work, hobbies, or interests. Students can create and ask interview questions.

6. The librarian brings in a collection of books about human diversity, and students share them in small groups, searching for answers to their questions.

7. As the students discover answers to their questions and learn any new information, this is recorded in the "L, What I Learned" section of the chart.

8. Finally, students fill out the Q, for more questions. This is an area where they ask more questions about the subject . . . the more one learns, the more questions one may have about the subject. Also, a literacy center on the subject may be set up specifically for the further study of human diversity.

9. Students write a research paper. The introduction begins with a paragraph about K. Then students write a paragraph about the three or four questions for which they are searching to find answers. In the next paragraph, students write about the answers to the questions asked. Then they end the research paper with questions for more study if they had more time. Each pair may write a paper, or individual papers may be assigned. Also, students may want to draw pictures to go with their papers. Last, students present their research to the whole class or in small groups.

Curriculum Connections

Any content area may be appropriate for this strategy. Diversity issues relate to biodiversity and ecology. A social studies curriculum concerning the world or the United States could include diversity studies. Mathematics may include diversity statistical information concerning averages, percentages, and graphs. Music and art are basics related to human diversity and associated with specific groups of people. Language arts classes naturally lend themselves to the reading, writing, listening, speaking, and viewing that occur in the KWLQ strategy for diversity study.

Teachers' Comments

"This helps my fifth graders understand how to structure research and appreciate differences at the same time."

"Comprehension of reading material improves with this approach."

"Students can work in pairs and learn together without the usual anxiety associated with research."

STRATEGY 45
Inquiry Learning: Questioning and Analysis

Traditionally, teachers have been the ones to ask questions in the classroom and students were required to answer the questions correctly. However, we know that the most effective classroom learning requires active involvement. Therefore, encouraging questioning and analysis of print and visual media produces students who are more capable of constructing meaning in any content area (Schmidt, 2001; Semali, 2001). These allow students to study different perspectives, perspectives that challenge mainstream thinking. As a result, students become more confident and are motivated as they design their inquiries for learning (Schmidt, 2001). Giving students opportunities for questioning provides a potential for seeing the relevance in learning. Students can then make applications to their own lives. KWLQ, "why do you think" questions, and Deep Viewing are ways to promote inquiry learning.

ELA Standard: 5 and 7

Here are a few examples of picture books that stimulate questioning:

Beginners and Intermediate Learners

Anno's (1977, 1983, 1996) wordless picture books create questioning about mathematics just by the nature of their illustrations.

City by the Numbers (1998) is a wordless math picture book that looks at common city sites and finds numbers present.

Encounter (1996) presents the discovery of the Western Hemisphere through the eyes of a Taino student.

Students of the World, Remember (1997) is a reminder for all concerning the beauty of our Earth and the need to care for it.

Advanced Learners

Terrible Things (1989) is an allegory of the Holocaust that is powerful and simple.

A River Ran Wild (1992) describes the evolution of a river from the time of the earliest settlers to the present day.

Hiroshima, No Pika (1980) is a story of survival by two women, who as students experienced the atomic bomb.

Why? (1996) is a wordless picture book that examines how conflict begins.

Smoky Nights (1999) gives a close-up look at the Los Angeles riots.

The Shaman's Apprentice (2001) demonstrates the need for collaboration between the old ways and the new ways in the Brazilian Amazon rain forest.

Storyteller's Beads (1998) tells of two teenage women's escape from the civil war in Ethiopia.

Curriculum Connections

Literature in the content area is a welcome change that can connect content areas for thematic instruction, thus demonstrating a cohesive curriculum. Students begin making connections between mathematics, science, and social studies when literature is used. When they see the connections, they can begin to see the world as a place for meaning making and diverse perspectives.

Teachers' Comments

"To get my kids to question can be a chore. This strategy stimulates questioning."

"Thematic instruction helps students see that we are all connected. Content diversity and population diversity go hand-in-hand."

"Literature stimulates, no matter what the content."

STRATEGY 46
Exploring Diversity on the Internet: Pen Pals and E-pals

This strategy employs the "traditional" practice of pen pals for communication in the electronic era, who may be called e-pals. Using e-mail, chat rooms, discussion boards, and other Internet-based forms of exchange and communication, the students correspond with other learners of a similar or different grade, region, language, or culture (Gallini & Helman, 1995; Shelley, 1996). This strategy may be used with a whole class or with individual students. To make this strategy successful, the teacher may need to learn the school policy regarding online access and school-approved sites for students. We strongly urge teachers to be very cautious when letting students use the Internet. Because of potential dangers involved in posting students' work on the Internet, the teacher needs to make sure that only pseudonyms are used, that no sensitive personal information is posted, and that any pictures and other personal information are posted only on a school-approved, password-protected site (cf. Strategy 8).

ELA Standards: 4 and 5

Beginning Learners

1. The teacher uses the school e-mail system for in-class or interclass communication.

2. As these students have not grasped enough vocabulary, the teacher may encourage the students to use common icons or symbols to represent full words, or help them spell difficult words.

Intermediate Learners

1. Repeat Steps 1–2.

2. One variation may be for the teacher to set up some kind of exchange program with another class at the same school or a different school to facilitate students' communication about issues they wonder about and would like to find out from their pen pals/e-pals.

Advanced Learners

1. The purpose and the steps of this pen pals/e-pals strategy need to be explained to the students clearly. Each student will compose a personal letter that introduces who he or she is and why the letter was written, providing information about his or her personal characteristics, school activities, interesting places in the city where the student lives, talents, favorite sports/foods/books/music, best friends, hobbies, interests, etc. This forms the first part of the letter to be sent out.

2. Next, the teacher will help the class brainstorm about things they wonder about and would like to find out about the lives of other students

who live in another part of the country or in a different country. Based on individual students' interests, those issues may be related to the topics from social studies, geography, or literature that the class has studied. Then, each student will need to add this part in the personal letter composed in Step 1.

3. The teacher may help students practice on the school-approved e-mail system. After this letter is composed, collect all students' e-mail addresses (if they don't already have one, help them set up one) to establish an e-mail distribution list. Then, ask each student to send the composed letter to the class. The recipients may respond with some suggestions for clarity and elaboration.

4. The teacher helps students post their letters on a school-approved safe site. If the teacher has personal contacts with teachers in other areas who have similar projects, the students' work may be exchanged via e-mail.

5. The key to the success of this strategy is continuity. After the initial round of contact, the teacher may encourage the students to keep up with writing to their pen pals/e-pals. As the communication continues and deepens, other topics or forms of communication may be explored.

Curriculum Connections

Print literacy and multimedia literacy are both important for students to learn. In addition, to increase the students' interests with specific topics covered in their social studies, geography, or literature classes, it may be helpful for them to be able to exchange and communicate directly with their peers from the particular region or culture. Besides communicating with other students, this strategy may also be employed for the students to contact a museum, a special magazine, or an organization for the relevant course-related information.

STRATEGY 47
Collecting Multicultural Adages

Students collect awe-inspiring sayings or adages from different countries and cultures. Adages are a reflection of wisdom and humor developed by different peoples. Studying these concise but meaningful expressions helps us get information about a culture or country. It is also a great way to develop literacy learning. For example:

Learning without thought means labor lost; thought without learning is perilous (Confucius);

Reading makes a full man, conference a ready man, and writing an exact man (Bacon);

We are the hero of our own story (McCarthy).

ELA Standard: 7

Beginning Learners

1. The teacher provides students with short adages related to children's life and interests, such as "A penny saved is a penny earned," or "Early to bed, early to rise, makes a man healthy, wealthy, and wise" (Franklin).

2. The teacher may lead the class to discuss the meanings and then recite and copy these and similar sayings.

Intermediate Learners

1. Repeat Steps 1–2.

2. The teachers asks students to search various sources, such as *Bartlett's Familiar Quotations*, collections of proverbs, multicultural readers, or the Internet, to look for more awe-inspiring adages.

Advanced Learners

1. The teacher first provides examples to explain what awe-inspiring adages are. For example: "Thinking is the talking of the soul with itself" (Plato); "The pen is the tongue of the mind" (Cervantes); "A man should so live as to be like a poem, a thing should so look as to be like a picture" (Zhang Chao).

2. The teacher and the students will discuss some of the sources for finding awe-inspiring adages. For example: *Encyclopedia of Proverbs, Encyclopedia of Famous Quotes, Oxford Dictionary of Proverbs*, etc.

3. Ask each student to collect at least 10 adages from around the world on the theme of education and learning.

4. Each student will present his or her adages to the whole class, explaining what these adages mean and why he or she likes them in particular.

5. After all the students have gathered their adages, the teacher and students may combine these adages into one volume as a class project, which may be called Awe-Inspiring Adages From Around the World.

Curriculum Connections

This strategy may be linked with the social studies and geography courses, particularly when the content involves different countries and cultures. In addition, it may be linked with English language arts and literature classes for literacy development.

STRATEGY 48
Multicultural Book Clubs

Research shows that when students have opportunities to respond to texts with personally invested meanings and to be exposed to multiple interpretations of others, they are more likely to be motivated in reading and their comprehension improves (Almasi, O'Flahavan, & Aray, 2001; Daniels, 2001; Evans, 2002; Goatley, Brock, & Raphael, 1995; McMahon & Raphael, 1997). While students may have come across writings about other cultures, this strategy provides opportunities for them to find a story from or about another culture or country to read. After reading the stories, students will form a discussion group to share the stories with other group members. Finally, each student will write a book report about what is read and what is understood and learned.

ELA Standards: 2 and 12

Beginning Learners

1. The teacher first selects a few stories from other cultures to read to the students to help them understand the many kinds of stories from other cultures and to arouse their interest in looking for a suitable book to read.

2. After the students have found and read their books, the teacher divides them into small groups of three or four students. Then, each group begins talking about their story.

3. The teacher may need to join each group to facilitate the discussion of the stories.

Intermediate Learners

1. Repeat Steps 1–3.

2. After each group finishes their talking and sharing, each student writes a short book report.

3. It is important not to overemphasize the written book report. The joy of reading and talking about the stories collaboratively must be promoted.

Advanced Learners

1. The teacher first shows the class a few stories from or about other cultures, such as African folktales, Chinese folktales, Indian folktales, European folktales, etc.

2. The students look for books that fall within the suggested categories. Based on themes or regions of the stories found by the students, the teacher divides the whole class into small reading groups of four students who will read the same book.

3. The students may take notes or write things they feel are interesting, puzzling, or in need of clarification.

4. Each reading group holds a discussion about the main ideas, setting, plot, characters, and theme of the book they read.

5. After the group discussion, the teacher invites volunteers from each group to talk about their stories to the whole class.

6. Each volunteer may briefly introduce the story and respond to questions from the audience. Next, the teacher may ask each group to prepare a written book report about the book they read. The book reports may be edited and combined into a volume called Interesting Folk Stories From Around the World.

Curriculum Connections

Literacy learning cannot be separated from actual reading. By combining book club with multicultural reading materials, students' literacy development is fostered through "conventional texts" in the English language arts and English literature classes. In addition, the multicultural contexts of the stories may help to enliven topics of social studies or geography classes while dealing with particular regions, periods, or peoples.

STRATEGY 49
Brain Teasers

This strategy makes use of print-based tricks or puzzles to expand students' literacy learning experiences and arouse their interest in trying to figure out the answers to puzzles that not only use language, but also involve logic and/or mathematical knowledge. Placing learning in a fun literacy environment may help the students (particularly ESL learners) to acquire useful vocabulary and develop their thinking.

ELA Standards: 3 and 12

Steps for Beginning Learners

1. The teacher begin, with the following warm-up question: "What is yours, but used by others more than yourself?" After the students figure out the answer (which is their *name*), the teacher may provide more visual examples to tease students' thinking. For example, the teacher asks the class: if a desk has four corners and you cut one corner off, how many corners are left? Some students may say THREE, FOUR, or FIVE. Instead of explaining verbally, the teacher may hold a regular piece of paper in hand, cuts one corner off with a pair of scissors to show students howmany corners are left.

2. Then, the teacher explains that brain teasers and puzzles such as the above ones ask for unconventional, unexpected, and often new ways of thinking about the problems.

3. Finally, the teacher gives the following teaser for students to solve. There are 11 wild birds in a tall maple tree. After one was shot down by a hunter, how many birds are thee in the tree? Students may be put in groups of fours, in which they explain their answer to each other. After the students complete their group sharing, the teacher may explain that, after one bird was shot dead, all the other birds would surely be all scared away. Therefore, instead of TEN, the answer is ZERO.

Steps for Intermediate Learners

1. Repeat Steps 1–3.

2. The teacher provides the following problem to students: A farmer has to cross a river to go to the market. He has a rooster, a dog and a bag of grain with him. As there is only one small boat to use that can take him and one of his belongs each time, the poor farmer was unsure how to cross the river. Remember, if left alone, the dog fight with the rooster, the rooster will eat the grain, but the dog will not eat the grain. Can you think of a way to help the farmer to cross the river with all his belongings safely?

3. The teacher should provide adequate time for the students to consider the problem and to figure out the answer. (The farmer would first take

the rooster to the other side of the river; he would return to take the dog (or grain) the second time but would take the rooster back with him; then he would leave the rooster but take the grain (dog) with him, again leaving the dog and the grain together. Finally, he would return to take the rooster with him. In case students cannot figure it all out by themselves, the teacher may provide some hints to guide their thinking (e.g., the dog and the rooster or the rooster and grain cannot stay together at any time, but the dog and the grain can).

Steps for Advanced Learners

1. Repeat the above Steps 1–3.

2. Then, the teacher asks students to visit at least one brain teaser web site (such as *http://www.flooble.com/perplexus; http://www. greylabyrinth.com; http://www.afunzone.com; http://www.syvum.com/ teasers*; etc.) to study additional brain teasers and puzzles.

3. The final step involves each student to create his or her own brain teaser problem in written form. The teacher divides the students into small groups of four, to share and to figure out each member's problem. Then, the teacher may facilitate the whole class to look at some of the fun problems together.

Curriculum Connections

This strategy combines literacy learning with creative thinking, logic and mathematical knowledge, and creative writing. This strategy also helps students to view and use these skills and knowledge as a cross-cultural tool for human thinking. The critical media component, such as online search of brain teaser websites and reading brain teasers from the websites, will further enhance their overall literacy development.

STRATEGY 50
Searching the Origins of English Words

This strategy involves the students in studying the origins of English words and phrases. As etymological awareness is probably still new to the students, this strategy will be used with small groups rather than with individual students. Checking etymological dictionaries in study groups, students may not only deepen their understanding of the particular expressions in question, but also develop an appreciation of the colorful history of the vocabulary, as well as the multicultural nature of the English language.

ELA Standard: 7

Steps for Beginning Learners

1. The teacher needs to clearly explain the purpose of this strategy. "Not all words that we take for granted as English expressions were always naturally in English. English has borrowed vocabulary from practically almost every language in the world. It is fun to know something about how certain expressions came into the language and became popular. For example, the word *school* came from Greek, which originally meant leisure; Santa Claus is a contraction of the Dutch 'Sant Nikolaas,' a patron saint of children; and hamburger took the name from the city of Hamburger, Germany. The purpose of this strategy is to help you learn the history behind some of the common words and expressions we use today."

2. As beginning learners are just starting to learn the spelling and meaning of vocabulary, instead of asking them to use dictionaries to check up the history of word(s), the teacher may ask the students to visually represent the word(s)' meaning. For example, students use sand to make a Hamburger, or using crayon to draw a Santa Claus, etc.

Steps for Intermediate Learners

1. Repeat Steps 1–2.

2. The teacher divides the class into study groups of 3-5 students. To begin with, the teacher supplies ten common words or phrases for all the groups to look up. A possible list, for example, may include the following: abracadabra, barbecue, hot dog, jihad, Marathon, palace, robot, tao, tsunami, skunk. (These *English* words or phrases originated from the following languages or countries: abracadabra, India; barbecue, Spanish; hot dog, U.S.; jihad, Arabic; Marathon, Greek; palace, French; robot, Czech; tao, Chinese; tsunami, Japanese; skunk, American Indian.)

3. In addition, each group will brainstorm ten more words or phrases to be added to teacher's list. Together, these twenty words will be the final list of words or expressions for that group to complete. After they look up

these words or expressions, each group will share their results with the class.

4. The teacher may suggest a few good etymological dictionaries for the students to use, such as *Klein's Comprehensive Etymological Dictionary of the English Language: Unabridged* (by Ernest Klein), *Oxford Dictionary of English Etymology* (by Charles T. Onions, Ed.), *The Encyclopedia of Word and Phrase Origins: Facts on File Series* (by Robert Hendrickson), and *2107 Curious Word Origins, Saying and Expressions: From White Elephants to Song Dance* (by Charles E. Funk).

Steps for Advanced Learners

1. Repeat the above steps 1-4.

2. After the search is completed, each group will make a presentation of their findings to the whole class. Each word or phrase needs to be explained in terms of why and how it orginated; where/when it was first used, and by whom; how the expression evolved over time; what the literal meanings were, and what they implied meanings are today; and any interesting stories associated with expression. Each group also needs to be prepared for answering questions from the audience

3. After the presentation, each group will prepare a written report about the results of their findings. Then, the teacher may put them together as a class project form a volume called *The Interesting Origins of some English Expressions.*

Curriculum Connections

Just as studying the spelling, grammar, genre, and other linguistic and formal aspects of the English language foster's students' literacy learning, their overall literacy development may be helped through learning the rich history of specific expressions. By studying the origins of certain "English" expressions, students may also begin to better understand how other cultures and peoples have contributed to the enrichment and development of the English language.

Conclusion

Now that you have tried these strategies, you may realize what other teachers, who worked on inservice programs with us, concluded "Indeed . . . there are seven characteristics for culturally responsive instruction and they can be described."

SEVEN CHARACTERISTICS FOR CULTURALLY RESPONSIVE INSTRUCTION (SCHMIDT, 2003)

When implementing successful culturally responsive instruction, teachers became aware of these specific characteristics. As they created lesson plans and observed videos of their classrooms, it became apparent that these *Seven*

1. High expectations—supporting students as they develop the literacy appropriate to their ages and abilities.

2. Positive relationships with families and community—demonstrating clear connections with student families and communities in terms of curriculum content and relationships.

3. Cultural sensitivity–reshaped curriculum—mediated for culturally valued knowledge, connecting with the standards-based curriculum as well as individual students' cultural backgrounds.

4. Active teaching methods—involving students in a variety of reading, writing, listening, speaking, and viewing behaviors throughout the lesson plan.

5. Teacher as facilitator—presenting information, briefly giving directions, summarizing responses, and working with small groups, pairs, and individuals.

6. Student control of portions of the lesson—"healthy hum"—talking at conversation levels around the topic studied while completing assignments in small groups and pairs.

7. Instruction around groups and pairs—low anxiety—completing assignments individually, but usually in small groups or pairs with time to share ideas and think critically about the work.

Characteristics were elements that provided a structure for assessing their own lesson plans. So, as you adapt the strategies in this book and create new ones, you may want to use the *Seven Characteristics* as your guide for success.

Additionally, when teachers in our inservice programs were asked to define culturally responsive teaching, they provided the list displayed below.

DEFINING CULTURALLY RESPONSIVE INSTRUCTION

One teacher said it best when explaining culturally responsive instruction: "Everybody benefits when there is culturally responsive teaching . . . children, families, teachers, and community." With this strong message, we conclude this book and wish you and your students, and their families and communities, the very best in education.

As you implement these 50 literacy strategies, think about how other teachers define culturally responsive instruction as expressed in the following box of statements.

- Teaching to and valuing the children's home and community experiences
- Participating in self-awareness and cross-cultural analyses exercises
- Talking frequently with family members
- Sharing portions of our personal lives with families
- Asking for help in obtaining community resources related to the curriculum
- Learning about community resources
- Sharing information for the child's education on a neutral or equal playing field
- Encouraging family involvement in the creation and implementation of inservice programs
- Creating lessons that include reading, writing, listening, speaking, and viewing and that connect home, school, and community

---

Epilogue

As we complete this text, we feel we have to respond to questions confronting most authors: So what? And what now?

First of all, and once again, this small collection of strategies aims at helping classroom teachers to enrich and diversify their literacy curricula across K–8 grades by offering some practical literacy learning strategies. Where applicable, we have offered suggestions for teaching across the curriculum. We have also connected specific content and ELA Standards with strategies. However, we want to emphasize again that the strategies are not intended to replace textbooks or standard curricula, thus they should not be directly linked to assessment in the content areas. (Although better command of content knowledge may result due to the connections made with students and their families and communities.) Actually, we believe these strategies may help teachers with additional ideas and activities to use, thus adding to more fun, engaging, and hands-on learning experiences for the students. We see these strategies as motivators and connectors to the standard curricula.

Moreover, we believe in teaching for diversity—cultural, ethnic/racial, linguistic, environmental, geographical, disciplinary, and conceptual, to name but a few. While teaching in the increasingly multicultural and complex world, it is all the more important to develop students' (and teachers') awareness of all forms of differences and similarities; of possibilities and hypotheses; of personal strengths and weaknesses; and of school, family, community, and society connections. We think such an open and multilateral view contributes to educating the learner not just with discrete skills and knowledge, but as a whole person with cognitive, social, and affective development. Needless to say, teaching about diversity does not magically rid the society of all problems and issues, but it is a necessary step to start facing and then addressing some of those concerns for a more accepting and just world. Teaching for these goals cannot be accomplished just by learning language skills or acquiring knowledge, nor does it end just by reading a few books. Yet the journey has to begin somewhere. We feel that the strategies included in this book may be a good place for some of our youngsters to begin.

In addition, even though we have used many of the strategies, or observed our colleagues using them, in actual classrooms or workshops at different points in our careers, the strategies are not written as summaries of empirical research. They are more of a reflection of our own (and our colleagues') classroom teaching experiences and exploration. We also want to point out that, although the strategies are clearly related to and supported by the theoretical framework that we presented at the beginning of the book regarding multicultural literacy, responsive pedagogy, and home/school connection for teaching and learning literacy and other content areas, we wrote the strategies in a simplified, step-by-step manner to make it easier for our teacher colleagues to operationalize any of them in their classrooms. Variations of some of the strategies may have been used in different classrooms, or recreated using other examples by ingenious teachers. In this sense, the strategies may appear simple, or not brand new. We still feel that putting them together in this book helps many more teachers to start the thinking and exploring process, as we did. This is particularly helpful to young teachers who have not yet accumulated many classroom-based strategies and are willing to try new ideas.

So, what's next? Of course the strategies included in this book are few, but they are useful for culturally responsive literacy instruction. They should not be viewed as fixed scripts. Classroom teachers are knowledgeable and resourceful, and they know their classrooms and students. While we learned from our own experiences that these strategies worked and would thus provide useful ideas for other teachers to implement in their literacy and cross-curriculum programs, it is up to each teacher who uses this book to view these strategies as works-in-progress—they may want to retest, modify, adapt, and/or recreate any of the strategies in order to better suit their instructional needs across different learners and learning contexts.

Resource A

Standards for the English Language Arts

In 1996, the International Reading Association and the National Council of Teachers of English published *Standards for the English Language Arts*. The document is the result of a project that involved thousands of educators, researchers, parents, policymakers, and others across the United States. Its purpose is to provide guidance in ensuring that all students are proficient language users so they may succeed in school, participate in society, find rewarding work, appreciate and contribute to our culture, and pursue their own goals and interests throughout their lives (www.reading.org/resources/issues/reports/learning_standards.html).

THE STANDARDS

1. Students read a wide range of print and nonprint texts to build an understanding of texts, of themselves, and of the cultures of the United States and the world; to acquire new information; to respond to the needs and demands of society and the workplace; and for personal fulfillment. Among these texts are fiction and nonfiction, classic and contemporary works.

2. Students read a wide range of literature from many periods in many genres to build an understanding of the many dimensions (e.g., philosophical, ethical, aesthetic) of human experience.

3. Students apply a wide range of strategies to comprehend, interpret, evaluate, and appreciate texts. They draw on their prior experience, their interactions with other readers and writers, their knowledge of word meaning and of other texts, their word identification strategies, and their understanding of textual features (e.g., sound-letter correspondence, sentence structure, context, graphics).

4. Students adjust their use of spoken, written, and visual language (e.g., conventions, style, vocabulary) to communicate effectively with a variety of audiences and for different purposes.

5. Students employ a wide range of strategies as they write and use different writing process elements appropriately to communicate with different audiences for a variety of purposes.

6. Students apply knowledge of language structure, language conventions (e.g., spelling and punctuation), media techniques, figurative language, and genre to create, critique, and discuss print and nonprint texts.

7. Students conduct research on issues and interests by generating ideas and questions, and by posing problems. They gather, evaluate, and synthesize data from a variety of sources (e.g., print and nonprint texts, artifacts, people) to communicate their discoveries in ways that suit their purpose and audience.

8. Students use a variety of technological and information resources (e.g., libraries, databases, computer networks, video) to gather and synthesize information and to create and communicate knowledge.

9. Students develop an understanding of and respect for diversity in language use, patterns, and dialects across cultures, ethnic groups, geographic regions, and social roles.

10. Students whose first language is not English make use of their first language to develop competence in the English language arts and to develop understanding of content across the curriculum.

11. Students participate as knowledgeable, reflective, creative, and critical members of a variety of literacy communities.

12. Students use spoken, written, and visual language to accomplish their own purposes (e.g., for learning, enjoyment, persuasion, and the exchange of information).

Resource B

List of Cited Youth Literature

Aliki, (1990). *Manners.* New York: Greenwillow.

Anderson, W. (1998). *Pioneer girl: The story of Laura Ingalls Wilder.* New York: HarperCollins.

Angelou, M. (1996). *Kofi and his magic.* New York: Clarkson Potter.

Anno, M. (1977). *Anno's journey.* Tokyo: Fukuinkan.

Anno, M. (1983). *Anno's mysterious multiplying jar.* New York: Philomel.

Anno, M. (2003) *Anno's Spain.* New York: Philomel.

Atkins, J. (1999). *Mary Anning and the sea dragon.* New York: Farrar, Straus, & Giroux.

Babbitt, N. (1975). *Tuck Everlasting* (34th printing). New York: Sunburst Books/Farrar, Straus, & Giroux.

Baker, K. (1997). *The magic fan.* Orlando, FL: Harcourt Brace.

Baker, O. (1985). *Where the buffaloes begin.* New York: Penguin Putnam.

Barbour, K. (1987). *Little Nino's pizzeria.* New York: Voyager.

Barracca, D. & S. (1990). *The adventures of taxi dog.* New York: Dial.

Belafonte, H., & Burgess, L. (2001). *Island in the sun.* New York: Penguin.

Bruchac, J. (1991). *Native American stories.* New York: Fulcrum.

Bryan, A. (2003). *All night, all day: A student's first book of African-American spirituals.* New York: Simon & Schuster.

Bunting, E. (1994). *How many days to America?* New York: Clarion.

Bunting, E. (1989). *Terrible things: Allegory of the holocaust.* New York: Jewish Publication Society of America.

Bunting, E. (1999). *Smoky nights.* New York: Voyager.

Burns, M. (1994). *The greedy triangle.* New York: Scholastic.

Burns, M. (1997). *Spaghetti and meatballs for all!* New York: Scholastic.

Cameron, A. (1993). *The most beautiful place in the world.* New York: Alfred A. Knopf.

Chang, M. (1997). *Story of the Chinese zodiac.* Taipei, Taiwan: Yuan-Liou.

Chao, L. (1987). *Stories from Mencius.* Beijing, Republic of China: The Overseas Chinese Library.

Cherry, L. (1992). *A river ran wild.* New York: Harcourt Brace.

Cherry, L. (1993). *The great kapok tree.* New York: Gulliver.

Cherry, L. (1999). *The armadillo from Amarillo.* New York: Voyager.

Cherry, L., & Plotkin, M. (2001). *Shaman's apprentice.* New York: Viking Press.

Climo, S. (1989). The *Egyptian Cinderella.* New York: Thomas Crowell.

Climo, S. (1993). *The Korean Cinderella.* New York: Thomas Crowell.

Climo, S. (1996). *The Irish Cinderlad.* New York: HarperCollins.

Climo, S. (1999). *The Persian Cinderella.* New York: HarperCollins.

Coburn, J. (1998). *Angkat: The Cambodian Cinderella.* Arcadia, CA: Shen's.

Coerr, E. (1993). *Sadako.* New York: G. P. Putnam's Sons.

Coles, R. (1995). *The story of Ruby Bridges.* New York: Scholastic.

Creech, S. (1994). *Walk two moons.* New York: HarperTrophy.

Dillon L., & Dillon, D. (1990). *Aida: Told by Leontyne Price.* New York: Gulliver.

Flake, S. (1999). *The skin I'm in.* New York: Hyperion.

Fox, M. (1997). *Whoever you are.* San Diego: Harcourt Brace.

Fox, P. (1991). *Monkey island.* New York: Yearling.

Garrett, A. (1999). *Keeper of the swamp.* New York: Publishers Group West.

Gleiter, J. (1989). *Diego Rivera.* New York: Raintree.

Grifalconi, A. (1986). *The village of round and square houses.* New York: Little, Brown.

Grutman J. H., & Matthaei, G. (1997). *The ledgerbook of Thomas Blue Eagle.* New York: Lickle.

Hearne, B. (1997). *Seven brave women.* New York: Greenwillow.

Heller, R. (1991). *More geometrics.* New York: Grosset & Dunlap.

Henkes, K. (1991). *Chrysanthemum.* New York: Greenwillow.

Hoose, P. (2001). *We were there, too!* New York: Farrar, Straus, & Giroux.

Hopkinson, D. (1995). *Sweet Clara and the freedom quilt.* New York: Alfred A. Knopf.

Hopkinson, D. (2003). *Girl wonder: A baseball story in nine innings.* New York: An Anne Schwartz Book.

Hopkinson, D. (2003). *Shutting out the sky.* New York: Orchard.

Isadora, R. (2002). *Caribbean dream.* New York: Scholastic.

Jaffe, N. (1996). *The golden flower.* New York: Simon & Schuster.

Jakobsen, K. (1993). *My New York.* New York: Little, Brown.

Jassem, K. (1987). *Sacajawea.* New York: Troll Associates.

Johnson, S. (1998). *City by numbers.* New York: Viking.

Kita, S. (1996). *Three whales who won the heart of the world.* Waipahu, HI: Island Heritage.

Kitsao, J. (1995). *McHeshi goes to the game park.* RioVista, CA: Jacaranda Designs.

Konisburg, E.I. (1996). *A view from Saturday.* New York: Simon & Schuster.

Kroll, V. (1992). *Masai and I.* New York: Simon & Schuster.

Krull, K. (1994). *Wilma unlimited.* San Diego: Harcourt Brace.

Kunin, C. (1993). *My Hanukkah alphabet.* New York: A Golden Book.

Kurtz, J. (1998). *The storyteller's beads.* San Diego: Harcourt Brace.

London, J. (1997). *Ali: Student of the desert.* New York: William Morrow.

Loomis, C. (2000). *Across America, I love you.* New York: Hyperion.

Lowry, L. (1993). *The giver.* Boston: Houghton Mifflin.

MacDonald, S. (1994). *Sea shapes.* New York: Gulliver.

Mahy, M. (1992). *The seven Chinese brothers.* New York: Scholastic.

Martin, J. B. (1998). *Snowflake Bentley.* Boston: Houghton Mifflin.

Maruki , T. (1980). *Hiroshima, No Pika.* New York: Lothrop, Lee & Shepherd.

Mayer, M. (1994). *Baba Yaga and Vasilisa the brave.* New York: Morrow Junior.

McGovern, A. (1992). *If You lived with the Sioux Indians.* New York: Scholastic.

Miller, W. (2000). *Tituba.* New York: Gulliver.

Moss, M. (2000). *Hannah's journal.* New York: Silver Whistle.

Murphy, S. J. (1997). *Betcha!* New York: Scholastic.

Murphy, S. J. (1997). *Divide and ride.* New York: HarperCollins.

Murphy, S. J. (1996). *Give me half!* New York: HarperCollins.

Musgrove, M. (1980). *Ashanti to Zulu: African traditions.* New York: Puffin.

Myers, W. D. (1997). *Harlem.* New York: Scholastic.

Myller, R. (1962). *How big is a foot?* New York: Bantam Doubleday Dell.

Neuschwander, C.(1997). *Sir Cumference and the first round table.* Watertown, MA: Charlesbridge.

Osofsky, A. (1992). *Dreamcatcher.* New York: Orchard.

Pack, L. (2002*). A is for Appalachia.* Prospect, KY: Harmony House.

Petit, J. (1996). *Maya Angelou: Journey of the heart.* New York: Puffin.

Polacco, P. (1988). *The keeping quilt.* New York: Simon & Schuster.

Popov, N. (1996). *Why?* New York: A Michael Neugebauer Book.

Provensen, A. (1995). *My fellow Americans.* New York: Browndeer Press.

Quiri, P. R. (1992). *The Algonquians.* New York: Franklin Watts.

Renner, M. (1999). *The girl who swam with the fish: Athabascan legend.* Vancouver, BC: Alaska Northwest.

Rhoads, D. (1993). *The corn grows ripe.* New York: Puffin.

Ringgold, F. (1988). *Tar Beach.* New York: Scholastic.

Ringgold, F. (1995). *My dream of Martin Luther King.* NewYork: Crown.

Rodanas, K. (1992). *Dragonfly's tale.* New York: Clarion.

Rohmer, H. (1997). *Just like me: Self-portraits of fourteen artists.* San Francisco: Students' Book Press.

Rohmer, H. (1999). *Honoring our ancestors: Stories and pictures by fourteen artists.* San Francisco: Students' Book Press.

Rosenblum. R. (1992). *Journey to the golden land.* Philadelphia: The Jewish Publication Society.

Sabuda, R. (1994). *Tutankamen's gift.* New York: Atheneum Press.

Sans Souci, R. D., & Perrault, C. C. (2001). *Cendrillon: A Caribbean cinderella.* New York: Simon & Schuster.

Say, A. (1993). *Grandfather's journey.* New York: Houghton Mifflin.

Schimmel, S. (1997*). Children of the earth . . . remember.* Minnetonka, MN: Northword Press.

Schwartz, D.(1985). *How much is a million.* New York: Scholastic.

Scieszka, J. (1995). *Math curse.* New York: Viking.

Selden, G. (1960). *Cricket in Times Square.* New York: Farrar, Straus, & Giroux.

Shelton, C. (1988). *San Antonio: The wayward river.* San Antonio, TX: San Antonio Press.

Sis, P. (1996). *Starry messenger.* New York: Farrar, Straus, & Giroux.

Sis, P. (1998). *Tibet: Through the red box.* New York: Farrar, Straus, & Giroux.

Speare, E. G. (1958). *Witch of Blackbird Pond.* New York: Houghton Mifflin.

Spier, P. (1980). *People.* New York: Delacorte Press.

Steptoe, J. (1987). *Mufaro's beautiful daughters: An African tale.* New York: Scholastic.

Stoutland, A. (1999). *Reach for the sky.* New York: Inch by Inch.

Strete, C. K. (1990). *Big thunder magic.* New York: HarperCollins.

Swope, S. (1989). *Araboolies of Liberty Street.* New York: Farrar, Straus, & Giroux.

Tan, A. (1992). *The moon lady.* New York: MacMillan.

Tang, G. (2001). *The grapes of math.* New York: Scholastic.

Tang, G. (2002). *Math for all seasons.* New York: Scholastic.

Tang, G.(2003). *Math-terpieces.* New York: Scholastic.

Tompert, A. (1990). *Grandfather Tang's story.* New York. Crown.

Unobagha,U. (2000). *Off to the sweet shores of Africa.* San Francisco: Chronicle.

Walters, C. (2001). *Play gently, Alfie bear.* New York: Dutton.

Wisniewski, D. (1991). *Rain player.* New York: Clarion.

Wong, J. S. (2000). *The trip back home.* Orlando, FL: Harcourt.

Wood, N. (1995). *Dancing moons.* New York: Doubleday.

Yarbrough, C. (1997). *Cornrows.* New York: Penguin Putnam.

Yep, L. (1975). *Dragonwings.* New York: HarperTrophy.

Yolen, J. (1990). *The devil's arithmetic.* New York: Puffin.

Yolen, J. (1996). *Encounter.* New York: Harcourt Brace.

References

Almasi, J. F., O'Flahavan, J. F., & Arya, P. (2001). A comparative analysis of student and teacher development in more and less proficient discussions of literature. *Reading Research Quarterly, 36*(2), 96–120.

Au, K. (1993). *Literacy instruction in multicultural settings.* New York: Harcourt Brace Jovanovich.

Banks, J. (1994). *An introduction to multicultural education.* Boston: Allyn & Bacon.

Barrera, R. B. (1992). The cultural gap in literature-based literacy instruction. *Education and Urban Society, 24*(2), 227–243.

Berkowitz, M. W. (1998). Finding common ground to study and implement charater education: Integrating structure and content in moral education. *Journal of Research in Education, 8*(1), 3–8.

Boykin, A. W. (1978). Psychological/behavioral verve in academic/task performance: Pre-theoretical considerations. *Journal of Negro Education, 47*(4), 343–354.

Boykin, A. W. (1984). Reading achievement and the social-cultural frame of reference of Afro-American students. *Journal of Negro Education 53*(4), 464–473.

Cazden, C. (2001). *Classroom discourse: The language of teaching and learning.* Portsmouth, NH: Heinemann.

Chaille, C., & Britain, L. (1991). *The young child as scientist: A constructivist approach to early childhood science education.* New York: HarperCollins.

Cochran-Smith, M. (1995). Uncertain allies: Understanding the boundaries of race and teaching. *Harvard Educational Review, 65*(4), 541–570.

Cummins, J. (1986). Empowering minority students: A framework for intervention. *Harvard Educational Review, 56*(1), 18–36.

Daniels, H. (2001). *Literature circles: Voice and choice in book clubs and reading groups,* 2nd ed. York, ME: Stenhouse Publishers.

Delpit, L. (1995). *Other people's students.* New York: The New Press.

Dewey, J. (1916). *Democracy and education: An introduction to the philosophy of education.* New York: MacMillan.

Edwards, P. A., Dandridge, J., McMillon, G. T., & Pleasants, H. M. (2001). Taking ownership of literacy: Who has the power?. In P. R. Schmidt & P. B. Mosenthal (Eds.), *Reconceptualizing literacy in the new age of multiculturalism and pluralism* (pp. 111–134). Greenwich, CT: Information Age Press.

Edwards, P. A., Pleasants, H., & Franklin, S. (1999). *A path to follow: Learning to listen to parents.* Portsmouth, NH: Heinemann.

Edwards, P. (2004). *Students' literacy development: Making it happen through school, family, and community involvement.* Boston: Allyn & Bacon.

Evans, K. (2002). Fifth-grade students' perceptions of how they experience literature discussion groups. *Reading Research Quarterly, 37*(1), 46–69.

Faltis, C. J. (1993, 2000). *Joinfostering: Adapting teaching strategies for the multilingual classroom.* New York: Maxwell Macmillan International.

Finkbeiner, C., & Koplin, C. (2002). A cooperative approach for facilitating intercultural education. *Reading Online, 6*(3). International Reading Association, www.reading online.org.

Florio-Ruane, S. (1994). The future teachers' autobiography club: Preparing educators to support learning in culturally diverse classrooms. *English Education, 26*(1), 52–56.

Foster, M. (1994). Effective black teachers: A literature review. In E. R. Hollins, J. E. King, & W. C. Hayman (Eds.), *Teaching diverse populations: Formulating a knowledge.* New York: SUNY.

Gallini, J. K., & Helman, N. (1995). Audience awareness in technology-mediated environments. *Journal of Educational Computing Research, 13*(3), 245–261.

Garcia, E. (2002). *Student cultural diversity: Understanding and meeting the challenge.* New York: Houghton Mifflin Company.

Gardner, H. (1999). *Intelligence reframed: Multiple intelligences for the 21st century.* New York: Basic Books.

Goatley, V. J., Brock, C. H., & Raphael, T. E. (1995). Diverse learners participating in regular education "Book Clubs." *Reading Research Quarterly, 30*(3), 352–380.

Goldenberg, C. N. (1987). Low-income Hispanic parents' contributions to their first-grade students' word-recognition skills. *Anthropology and Education Quarterly, 18,* 149–179.

Greene, S., & Abt-Perkins, D. (2003). *Making race visible.* New York: Teachers College Press.

Heath, S. B. (1983). *Ways with words: Language life and work in communities and classrooms.* Cambridge, UK: Cambridge University Press.

Herber, H. L. (1978). *Teaching reading in content areas* (2nd ed.). Upper Saddle River, NJ: Prentice Hall.

Hopkinson, D. (2001). Historical fiction picture books and values: An author's reflections. In P. Ruggiano Schmidt & A. Watts Pailliotet (Eds.) *Exploring values through literature, multimedia, and literacy events.* Newark, DE: International Reading Association.

Howard, T. (2001). Telling their side of the story: African American students' perceptions of culturally relevant teaching. *The Urban Review, 33*(2), 131–149.

Hynds, S. (1997). *On the brink: Negotiating literature and life with adolescents.* Newark, DE: Teachers College Press/International Reading Association.

Igoa, C. (1995). *The inner world of the immigrant student.* Mahwah, NJ: Lawrence Erlbaum.

Jensen, R. (2005). *The heart of whiteness.* San Francisco: City Lights.

Kurtz, J. (2001). Multicultural books and values: Connecting with people and places. In P. Ruggiano Schmidt & A. Watts Pailliotet (Eds.), *Exploring values through literature, multimedia, and literacy events.* Newark, DE: International Reading Association.

Ladson-Billings, G. (1994). *The dreamkeepers: Successful teachers of African American students.* San Francisco: Jossey-Bass.

Ladson-Billings, G. (1995). Toward a theory of culturally relevant pedagogy. *American Educational Research Journal, 32,* 465–491.

Laier, B. B., Edwards, P. A., McMillon, G. T., & Turner, J. D. (2001). Connecting home and school values through multicultural literature and family stories. In P. R. Schmidt & A. W. Pailliotet, *Exploring values through literature, multimedia, and literacy events.* Newark, DE: International Reading Association.

Lalik, R., & Hinchman, K. (2001). Critical issues: Examining constructions of race in literacy research: Beyond silence and other oppressions of white liberalism. *Journal of Literacy Research, 33*(3), 529–561.

Leftwich, S. (2002). Learning to use diverse students' literature in the classroom: A model for preservice teacher education. *Reading Online, 6*(2). International Reading Association, www.readingonline.org

McCaleb, S. P. (1994). *Building communities of learners.* New York: St. Martin's Press.

McGovern, M. (1997). *Starting small* (video). 400 Washington Ave, Montgomery, AL: Teaching Tolerance.

McIntosh, P (1990). *White privilege: Unpacking the invisible knapsack. Independent School,* Wellesley College Winter Issue. Wellesley, MA.

McMahon, S., & Raphael, T. (Eds.). (1997). *The book club connection: Literacy, learning, and classroom talk.* New York: Teachers College Press.

Moll, L. C. (1992). Bilingual classroom studies and community analysis: Recent Trends. *Educational Researcher, 21*(2), 20–24.

Morris, D., Bloodgood, J., & Perney, J. (2003). Kindergarten predictors of first- and second-grade reading achievement. *Elementary School Journal, 104*(2), 93–110.

Nieto, S. (1999). *The light in their eyes.* New York: Teachers College Press.

Noordhoff, K., & Kleinfield, J. (1993). Preparing teachers for multicultural classrooms. *Teaching and Teacher Education, 9*(1), 27–39.

Ogle, D. (1986). KWL: A teaching model that develops active reading of expository text. *The Reading Teacher, 39,* 564–570.

Osborne, A. B. (1996). Practice into theory into practice: Culturally relevant pedagogy for students we have marginalized and normalized. *Anthropology and Education Quarterly, 27* (3), 285–314.

Pailliotet, A. W. (2001). Critical media literacy and values: Connecting the 5 W. In P. R. Schmidt & A. W. Pailliotet (Eds.), *Exploring values through literature, multimedia, and literacy events* (pp. 20–45). Newark, DE: International Reading Association.

Paley, V. G. (1989). *White teacher.* Cambridge, MA: Harvard University Press.

Pattnaik, J. (1997). Cultural stereotypes and preservice education: Moving beyond our biases. *Equity and Excellence in Education, 30*(3), 40–50.

Payne, R. K., DeVol, P., & Smith, T. D. (2005). *Bridges out of poverty.* Aha! Process Highlands, TX:.

PBS Adult Learning Service (1999). *Scanning television* (video). Alexandria, VA: Face to Face Media Limited.

Purcell-Gates, V., L'Allier, S. & Smith, D. (1995). Literacy at the Harts' and the Larsons': Diversity among poor inner-city families. *The Reading Teacher, 48*(7), 572–578.

Reyhner, J. & Garcia, R. L. (1989). Helping minorities read better: Problems and promises. *Reading Research and Instruction, 28*(3), 84–91.

Risko, V. J. & Bromley, K. (Eds.). *Collaboration for diverse learners: Viewpoints and practices.* Newark, DE: IRA.

Rosenblatt, L. M. (1982). The literacy transaction: Evocation and response. *Theory Into Practice, 21,* 268–277.

Rumelhart, D. E. (1982). Schemata: The building blocks of cognition. In J. Guthrie (Ed.), *Comprehension and teaching: Reseach reviews.* Newark, DE: International Reading Association.

Schmidt, P. R. (1998a). *Cultural conflict and struggle: Literacy learning in a kindergarten program.* New York: Peter Lang.

Schmidt, P. R. (1998b). The ABC's of cultural understanding and communication. *Equity and Excellence in Education, 31*(2), 28–38.

Schmidt, P. R. (1998c). The ABC's Model: Teachers connect home and school. In T. Shanahan & F. V. Rodriguez-Brown (Eds.), *National reading conference yearbook 47* (pp. 194–208.). Chicago, IL: National Reading Conference.

Schmidt, P. R. (1999a). KWLQ: Inquiry and literacy learning in science. *The Reading Teacher, 52*(6), 789–792.

Schmidt, P. R. (1999b). Know thyself and understand others. *Language Arts, 76*(4), 332–340.

Schmidt, P. R. (2000a). Emphasizing differences to build cultural understandings. In V. Risko and K. Bromley (Eds.), *Collaboration for Diverse Learners: Viewpoints and Practices.* Newark, DE: IRA.

Schmidt, P. R. (2000b). Teachers connecting and communicating with families for literacy development. In T. Shanahan & F. Rodriguez-Brown (Eds.), *National Reading Conference Yearbook, 49.* Chicago: National Reading Conference.

Schmidt, P. R. (2001). The power to empower. In P. R. Schmidt & P. B. Mosenthal (Eds.). *Reconceptualizing literacy in the new age of multiculturalism and pluralism.* Greenwich, CT: Information Age Press.

Schmidt, P. R. (2002). Literacy learning and scientific inquiry: Students respond. *The Reading Teacher, 55*(6), 534–548.

Schmidt, P. R. (2003). Balance is beautiful. In P. Mason & J. Schumm (Eds.). *Promising practices for urban reading instruction.* Newark DE: International Reading Association.

Schmidt, P. R. (2004, December). *Supporting culturally relevant pedagogy: It made the difference.* Paper presented at the annual meeting of the National Reading Conference, San Antonio, TX.

Schmidt, P. R. (2005). *Preparing educators to communicate and connect with families and communities.* Greenwich, CT: Information Age.

Schmidt, P. R., & Pailliotet, A. W. (2001). *Exploring values through literature, multimedia and literacy events.* Newark, DE: International Reading Association.

Schon, D. (1987). *Educating the reflective practitioner.* San Francisco: Jossey-Bass.

Semali, L. M. (1999). Critical viewing as a response to intermediality: Implications for media literacy. In L. M. Semali & A. W. Pailliotet (Eds.). *Intermediality: The teachers' handbook of critical media literacy* (pp. 1–30). Boulder, CO: Westview.

Semali, L. (2001). Unraveling the curriculum of global values. In P. Schmidt & A. Watts Pailliotet (Eds.), *Exploring values through literature, multimedia, and literacy events.* Newark, DE: International Reading Association.

Shananan, T., & Rodriguez-Brown, V. F. (Eds.). *National reading conference yearbook 47,* 194–208. Chicago: National Reading Conference.

Shelley, J. O. (1996). Minneapolis and Brittany: Children bridge geographical and social differences through technology. *Learning Languages, 2*(1), 3–11.

Siegler, R. S., & Alibali, M. W. (2005). *Children's thinking: International edition,* 4e. New York: Prentice Hall.

Slavin, R. E. (1990). *Cooperative learning: Theory, research, and practice.* Englewood Cliffs, NJ: Prentice Hall.

Sleeter, C. E. (2001). Preparing teachers for culturally diverse schools. *Journal of Teacher Education, 52*(2), 94–106.

Snyder, T. D., Hoffman, C. M., & Geddes, C. M. (1997). *Digest of education statistics.* Washington, DC. National Center of Education Statistics, Office of Educational Research and Improvement.

Tatum, A. (2000). Breaking down barriers that disenfranchise African American Adolescent readers in low-level tracks. In P. Mason & J. S. Schumm (Eds.), *Promising practices for urban reading instruction* (pp. 98–118). Newark, DE: International Reading Association.

Tatum, B. (1992). Talking about race, learning about racism: The application of racial identity theory in the classroom. *Harvard Educational Review, 62*(1), 1–24.

Tatum, B. (1997). *Why are all the black kids sitting together in the cafeteria?* New York: Basic Books.

Trueba, H. T., Jacobs, L. & Kirton, E. (1990). *Cultural conflict and adaptation: The case of the Hmong students in American society.* New York: Falmer Press.

U.S. Department of Education. (2000). *Minority population growth.* Washington, DC: U.S. Department of Education.

Walker-Dalhouse, D., & Dalhouse, A. D. (2001). Parent–school relations: Communicating more effectively with African American parents. *Young Students,* 75–80.

Wallace, B. (2000). A call for change in multicultural training at graduate schools of education: Educating to end oppression and for social justice. *Teachers College Record, 102*(2), 1086–1111.

Watson, M., & Ecken, L. (2003). *Learning to trust: Transforming difficult elementary classrooms through developmental discipline.* San Francisco: Jossey-Bass.

Willis, A. I., & Meacham, S. J. (1997). Break point: The challenges of teaching multicultural education courses. *JAEPL, 2,* 40–49.

Xu, H. (2000). Preservice teachers in a literacy methods course consider issues of diversity. *Journal of Literacy Research, 32*(4), 505–531.

Zeichner, K. M. (1993). *Educating teachers for cultural diversity.* East Lansing, MI: National Center on Teacher Learning.

Index